Mel Bay's Master Anthology of

BLUES GUITAR SOLOS

volume one

Featuring solos by the world's finest blues guitarists!

D0989165

2 3 4 5 6 7 8 9 0

Visit us on the Web at www.melbay.com — E-mail us at email@melbay.com

Contents

Muriel Anderson

Muriel Anderson was raised in a musical family in Downers Grove, Illinois, USA. Her mother taught piano and her grandfather had played saxophone in John Philip Sousa's band. Muriel fell in love with the guitar at age ten and learned every style available to her, culminating in classical guitar study at DePaul University. She went on to study with classical virtuoso Christopher Parkening and with Nashville legend Chet Atkins. In 1989 Muriel won the National Fingerpicking Guitar Championship.

Muriel Anderson has released several CDs: Heartstrings, *Arioso From Paris, Hometown Live, A Little Christmas Gift (*CGD Music) with French guitarist Jean-Felix Lalanne and *Le Duet* (Rarefied Records). Muriel's *Heartstrings* cassette accompanied the astronauts into orbit on a Space Shuttle mission, traveling some 2.5 million miles.

She has released an instructional video with Homespun Tapes: *The Techniques and Arrangements of Muriel Anderson* and instructional guitar book: *Building Guitar Arrangments From the Ground Up, All Chords In All Positions* (Hal Leonard Pub.), *Muriel Anderson Hometown Live* (Mel Bay, MB95664BCD). Muriel writes for several guitar magazines and teaches guitar at Belmont University in Nashville.

She originated and hosts *"Muriel Anderson's All Star Guitar Night"* and has performed at Orchestra Hall in Chicago, the Ryman Auditorium and the Grand Ole Opry in Nashville, Tennessee, and the Olympia Theater in Paris.

Blues for Macedonia

This begins in a loose Macedonian 7/8 time. It is counted as a long beat followed by two short beats. The long beat corresponds to three eighth notes and the short beats correspond to two eighth notes. Instead of counting a very quick 1-2-3, 1-2, 1-2, or 1-2, 1, 1-2, 1-2, (for a total of seven beats) you can count it as simply long-and-short-short. The "and" corresponds to the eighth note in the bass on beat three. You can also think of the timing as a variation of 4/4 time, where beat two is shorter than the other beats (an eighth note instead of a quarter note). Within that rhythmic scheme, allow the rhythm to pull back with slight trepidation on the two quarter notes leading into the Bm7-5 chords and E7 chords, as in measures 27 and 35. Measures 62 and 63 go briefly into a walking-rhythm, more like a 4/4, then back to the dance-like quality of the 7/8.

The rhythm changes abruptly to a 4/4 blues at measure 74, then a brief revisitation of the 7/8 at measure 90.

Blues for Macedonia

Muriel Anderson

♪ = 280
Loose 7/8

© 1999 Muriel Anderson, Heartstrings Attached Music, BMI

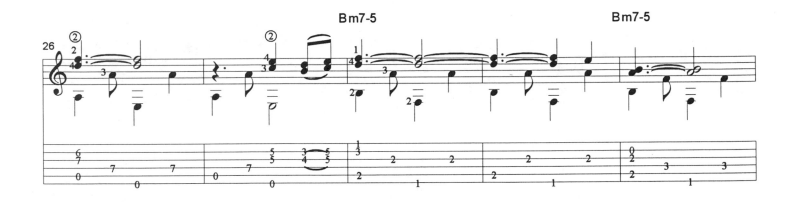

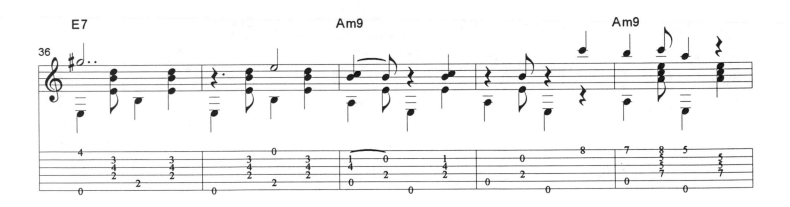

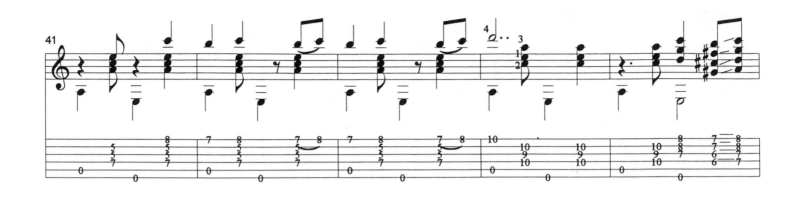

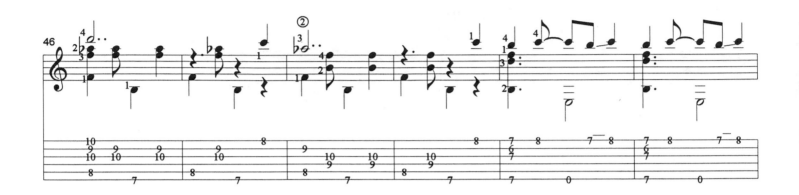

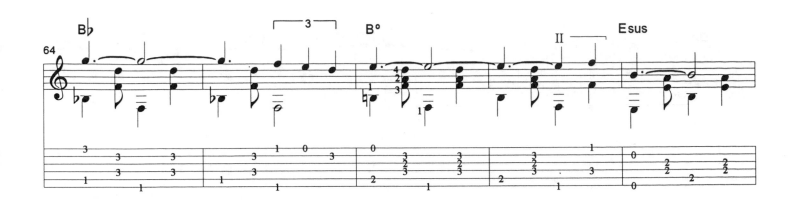

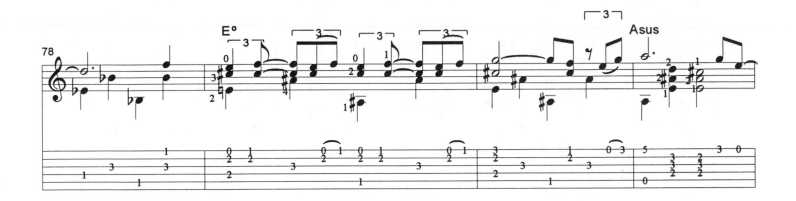

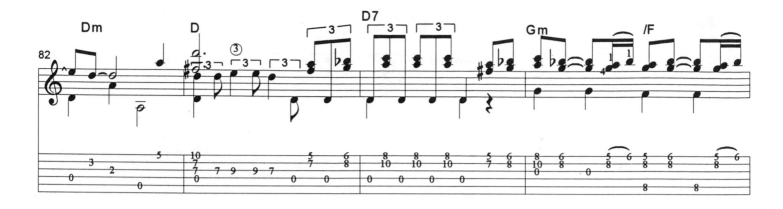

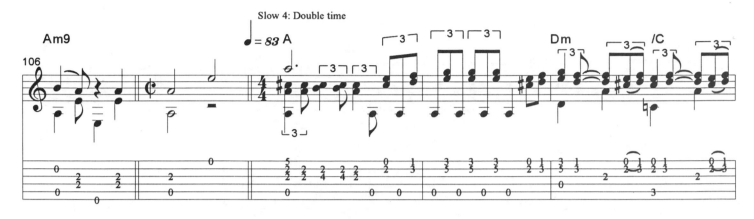

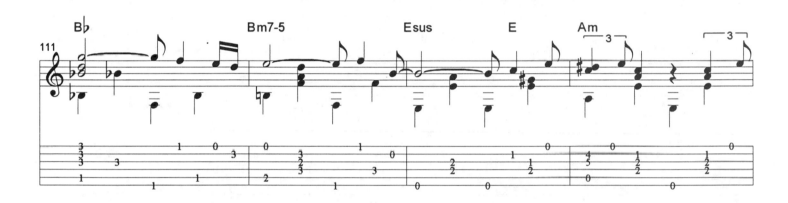

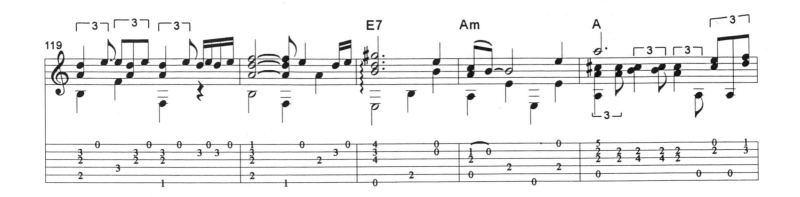

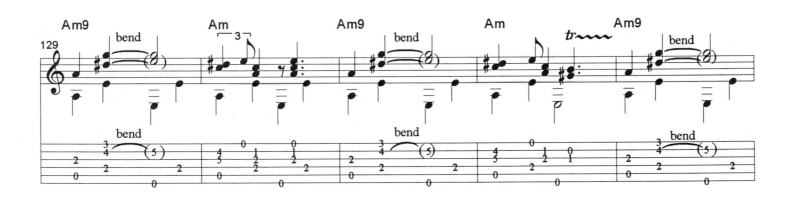

Duck Baker

Duck Baker was born Richard R. Baker IV in Washington, D.C. in 1949 and grew up in Richmond, Virginia. His teenage years were devoted to playing in rock and blues bands before becoming interested in fingerpicking in local coffeehouses. Ragtime pianist Buck Evans was a major influence on Baker's developing interests, which by the time he moved to San Francisco in 1973 included rags, blues, old-time country, Cajun, bluegrass and New Orleans jazz. This variety inspired the title of his first solo record, *There's Something for Everyone in America*, released by Kicking Mule Records in 1976.

During the next four years, Baker recorded four more solo records, including one devoted to swing, one to modern jazz and one to Irish and Scottish tunes, and appeared on nine others. He also wrote a book of fiddle tune arrangements and toured incessantly throughout America, Canada, Europe, and Australia. He changed address almost as constantly, finally winding up in Europe for most of the '80s. He returned to San Francisco in 1987 and finally to Virginia in 1991. Most of his more recent solo recordings have featured his own compositions, an aspect of his work that has drawn particular praise from other guitarists.

If Baker's insistence on studying and performing so many facets of folk and related musics, from medieval European carols to avant-garde jazz, have made him somewhat difficult for the press to categorize, he certainly has earned the respect of his peers. A check list of musicians with whom he has been associated professionally (in performance or on records) would include bluesmen Charlie Musselwhite and Jerry Ricks, bluegrassers Tim O'Brien and Dan Crary, traditionalists Ali Anderson and Brian MacNeil, new music icon John Zorn, rock legend J.J. Cale, and jug band king Jim Kweskin. His fingerpicking peers are on records as saying:

"Duck Baker is a true genius of guitar." —Stefan Grossman

"Duck has discovered a way to write which is purely and originally beautiful. I think he sets a standard we all can aspire to." —Leo Kottke

"I suspect that Duck's compositions will make a significant contribution to the repertoire of the guitar, but until then the music makes fantastic listening." —John Renbourn

Still Staggerin'

"Still Staggerin'" uses a chord progression that moves around the circle of fifths: E-C#7 - F#m7 - B7 in one case, A - F#7 - B7 - E7 in the other. If these chords are unfamiliar, remember that in C or G, the progression would be C - A7 - D7 - G7 or G - E7 - A7 - D7. Actually, "Still Staggerin'" is an interesting progression all the way through. It's based on Jerry Ricks' version of "Stagger Lee," which is based on several others. Hence the title.

This one starts with familiar shapes for the first few bars. At the end of bar 5 and into bar 6 are two F# chords:

 and

Bar 7 features a pull-off that changes a B9 to a familiar diminished shape:

The trick is laying the index finger down for the half-bar on the 1st fret without losing the sound of the note it was holding on the 4th string. This is somewhat difficult but something we need to be able to do in advanced playing.

This tune features a hook in bars 13-14 that goes from A to D to A to F#+5. There are several ways to finger this last chord, but I use:

We begin bar 15 with a B9, and then the pinkie has to stretch to the 4th fret, 4th string, without the ring and middle fingers moving. If this phrase sounds familiar, it's been used in dozens of songs, from "Fishin' Blues" to "I'm Beginning to See the Light" to "I've Got the Hongries for Your Love and I'm Waitin' in Your Welfare Line."

Start with your left index and ring fingers and then slide your ring finger from the 4th fret of the 3rd string up to the 6th. Get the next two notes on the 2nd string with the middle and little fingers. If you make a full bar on the 4th fret with your index finger, the rest of bar 2 should fall into place.

The key to bars 4-5 is that the middle finger stays anchored at the 6th fret of the 3rd string once it gets there. Also note that the index finger doesn't bar the three high strings but moves from one to the other. We wind up in bar 6 with the index finger on the 5th fret, 2nd string, the middle finger still holding the 6th fret of the 3rd, and the thumb reaching around for the bass note on the 6th fret of the low string. Then the index and middle fingers walk their way down the frets until they get to the 2nd and 3rd, while the thumb jumps ahead to the 2nd fret. This is awkward but not as hard as it may seem at first. The next few bars are familiar shapes.

Variation 3 is based on chord riffs alternating with high-string runs in what's called a call-and-response pattern. The A7 and D7 shapes in bar 1 should be familiar, but notice the trick of putting the E bass under the D7—you can get a lot of mileage out of that. The melody notes in bar 2 are all fretted with the ring and index fingers, and the rest of the runs shouldn't be hard to work out until late in bar 6, when the index finger goes to the 6th fret of the 3rd string so that the middle finger can slide from the 7th fret to the 8th as we come into bar 7. When it gets there we need to have a full bar down on the 7th fret, which puts us in position for the B9 and E7 that follow. Similarly, in bars 10-11, the little finger slides up the 2nd string from the 6th to the 7th fret as the index finger bars the 5th fret.

Our hook is now an octave higher, so we need to work out of:

For the D that follows, the index and middle fingers stay where they are while the little finger moves over to the high string. The C9 shape that follows in bar 14 is used as a substitute for F#+5.

The last variation gets back to alternating bass lines in shapes we've seen by now. Note that the 12HP1PO figure in bar 4 is out of a normal A7, and bars 5-6 are a bar chord.

Still Staggerin'

Duck Baker

Used by Permission

14

15

Play the 1st time

Coda the 2nd time

D.S.
Al
Coda

✱ These four bars function as the coda
after the D.S.

Mickey Baker

Mickey Baker's reputation amongst many guitarists is mainly as an author of various guitar books and tutors. But he has also been a professional guitarist mainly in the field of Rhythm and Blues music. He is still musically active but now lives in Paris with his wife Sylvia.

As a boy Baker lived in an orphanage and it was in this institution's marching band that he first developed an interest in music. At the age of sixteen he ran away from the orphanage and ended up in New York paying his way as a laborer. By the time he was nineteen, having listened to many leading jazz musicians, including Charlie Parker and Dizzy Gillespie, Baker decided that he wanted to be a jazz musician. The trumpet was his first choice but the finance needed to purchase this instrument was too high, so at the age of nineteen he decided to buy a guitar.

After a few years study, including a short spell at the New York School of Music, Mickey Baker developed the ability, in 1949, to form his own jazz group. This venture was not a financial success so he decided to move to California. There the reception to his progressive style of jazz music was even less successful. While he was trying to earn the money needed to get back to New York Baker heard blues guitarist, Pee Wee Creighton. He liked what he heard and saw that Creighton was earning a good living. The result was that Baker changed his guitar style and returned to New York as a blues guitarist. His decision proved correct as Mickey Baker, blues guitarist, found himself much in demand for the Atlantic. Savoy and King labels as a backing artist for top blues artists, including Ray Charles, Big Joe Turner, Ruth Brown, and The Drifters.

During the mid 1950s Baker felt he could improve his financial status by emulating the chart topping duo of guitar wizard Les Paul and singer Mary Ford. He joined forces with an ex-student of his named Sylvia and in 1957 they had a smash hit with a song called 'Love is Strange.' Their popularity was to last right through to 1961. With this success behind them the Bakers were financially able to establish their own publishing and recording companies, as well as their own nightclub.

Since the early 1950s Mickey Baker had been working on his tutors and music albums and now through his own publishing company, he was able to achieve worldwide distribution for these works.

Despite his success as a blues and popular guitarist Baker felt that he still wished to play jazz guitar again. He therefore decided to move with his wife to Europe where he hoped he could develop a more fulfilling musical life.

He bought a home in Paris and established permanent French residency there. Since that time Mickey Baker has prospered writing, arranging, leading various groups and has to a great extent fulfilled his desire to continue playing his own distinctive style of jazz and blues guitar.

Alley Music
(Blues)

Used by Permission

* Recording ends here

push

B

push

19

Carlos Barbosa-Lima

Born in 1944 in São Paulo, Brazil, Carlos Barbosa-Lima began studying the guitar at the age of seven, making his concert debut five years later in São Paulo and Rio de Janeiro. Since his United States debut in 1967, Mr. Barbosa-Lima has enjoyed a global concert career marked by numerous distinguished recordings. The breadth of his repertoire and his unique ability to integrate diverse musical styles are strong features of his work.

St. Louis Blues

Arr: by John Griggs
and Carlos Barbosa-Lima (BMI)

⑤ - G
⑥ - D

Moderate Blues

23

24

William Bay

William Bay is president of Mel Bay Publications, Inc. He began playing the trumpet at the age of 5 and became an accomplished soloist featured with bands and orchestras throughout the St. Louis area. For years, he led his own jazz orchestra. Bill is also a fine guitarist who has performed in a wide variety of professional musical settings. He received his undergraduate degree from Washington University in St. Louis and his master's degree from the University of Missouri/Columbia. Bill has written over 100 books dealing with a wide assortment of musical topics, instruments, and proficiency levels, with sales in the millions.

Blue Dawn

Fingerstyle or Flatpick Solo
Slowly, with a beat

William Bay

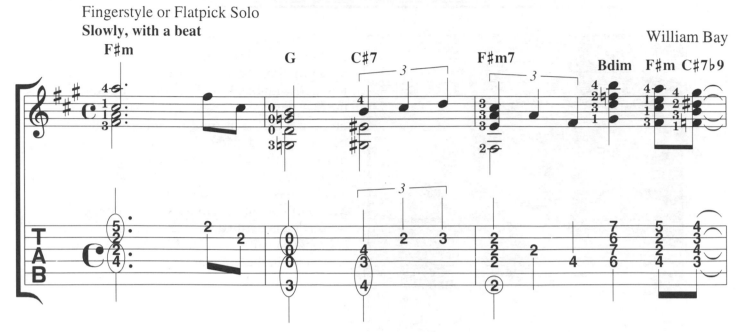

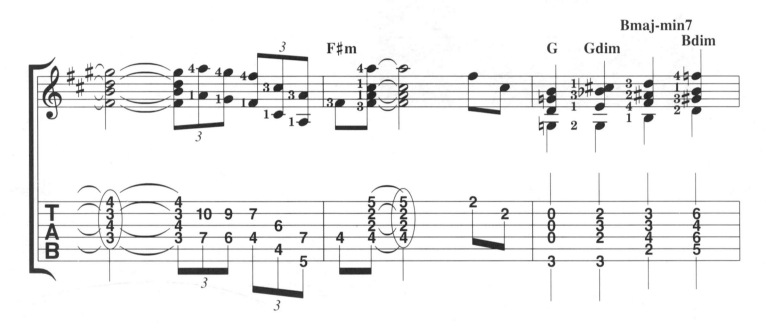

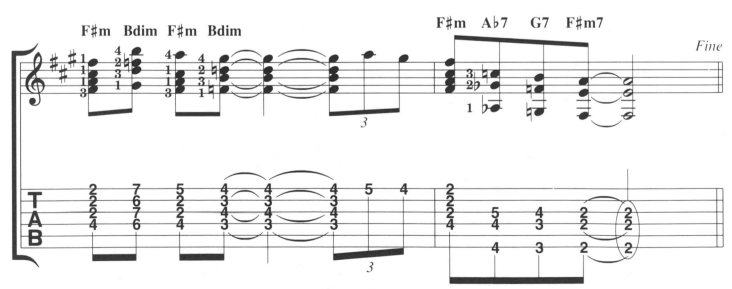

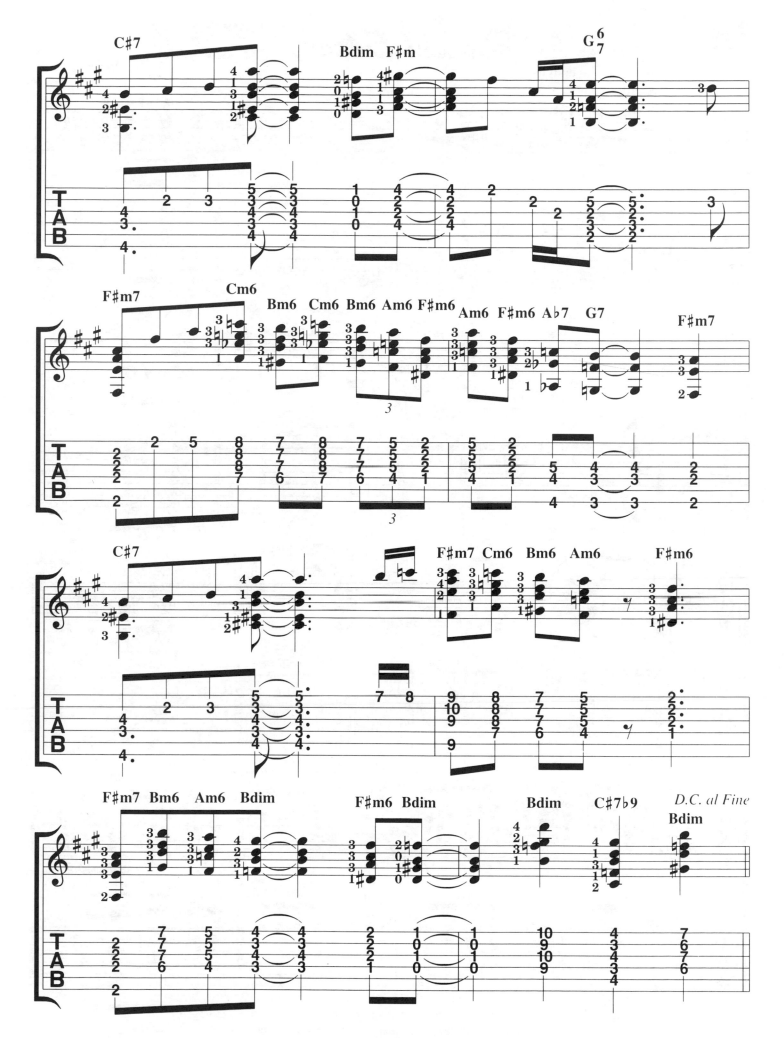

29

Russel Street

William Bay

Flatpick or Fingerstyle
Slow, bluesy

♩ = 90

A♭6

Larry Bolles

Guitarist Larry Bolles grew up in a musical household. His parents played equal amounts of popular and classical music. He studied piano and trombone before falling in love with the guitar at the age of 21. His first lessons consisted of copying recordings of acoustic players such as John Lee Hooker, Leo Kottke, and John Renbourn. He went on to study classical and jazz guitar at Washington University and Webster University in St. Louis. After graduating from Webster University he was made head of their classical guitar department where he taught for ten years. He went on to help found The Musical Arts Academy where guitarists can combine their studies of classical and popular music. Larry now divides his time between teaching, performing, and composing music in a variety of styles.

"*Icicle Blues* is the only piece I have written with a date attached to the title – Jan, 10, 1993. After days of ice I had to use a hammer and chisel to make a path for guitar students to walk to my studio. At the end of that day this song begged to be written." Your input welcomed at: <lbolles@my-deja.com.>

Icicle Blues

Larry Bolles

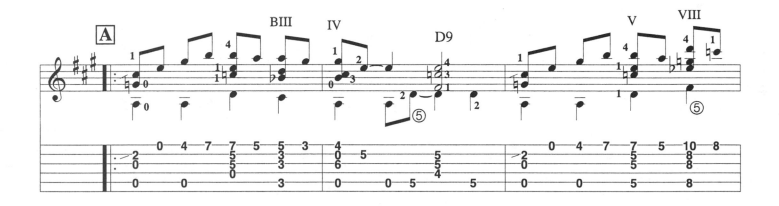

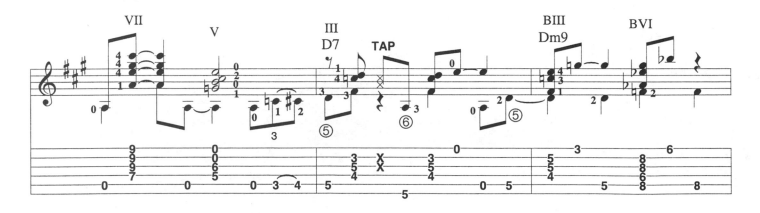

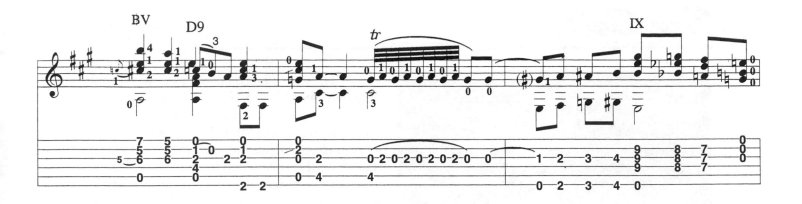

D.C. al Coda

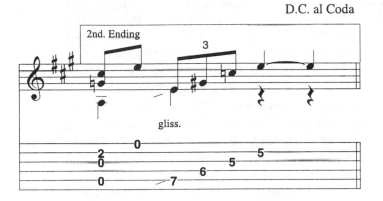

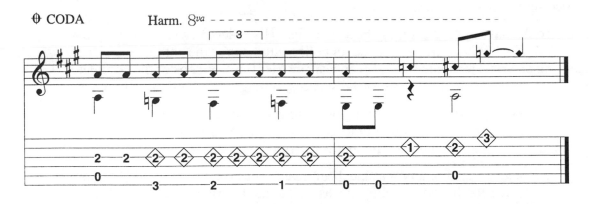

Note: 1st. Ending repeats to [A]. 2nd. Ending goes to start until: To ⊕.
All harmonics are artificial, right hand touches 12 frets above fretted note.

Ben Bolt

Ben Bolt is credited with being the first classical guitarist to introduce thousands of new people to the classical style of guitar through his videos and books, which use a revolutionary format of learning. In the past, guitar students needed to learn to read music at the same time they were learning to play the guitar, which was complicated. Since the publication of Bolt's book/tape packages, beginners are able to play immediately. The tablature, using lines and numbers to show where the notes are, and the tape, which is rhythmically self-explanatory, empowers all students to play. Bolt's work has been mimicked throughout the publishing world. Because of his vision of making classical guitar accessible to all kinds of musicians, the classic guitar is being experienced by the masses.

Andrés Segovia, the father of classical guitar, said, "Ben Bolt is an excellent guitarist with fine tone." Segovia personally paid for a scholarship so that Bolt could continue his studies at the Musica en Compostela, which Segovia had founded. During the Spanish Civil War Segovia had been in exile in Montevideo, Uruguay. He was not concertizing in Europe, due to World War II. Because of extra time, he took on one of his most talented students, Abel Carlevaro. Carlevaro took lessons every other day for over ten years in Uruguay. Because of this historic fact, Bolt sought out Carlevaro in order to attain more information about Segovia. In Paris Bolt studied with Maestro Carlevaro, who wanted to continue teaching Bolt in Brazil at the International Guitar Conservatory. There, under full scholarship Bolt was introduced to more Segovia information, but equally important, the Carlevaro school of technique. During the next several years he went on to Montevideo, Carlevaro's hometown, and completed his music studies under the direction of Maestro Carlevaro and Guido Santorsola, the distinguished Italian composer and conductor.

Several Ben Bolt books have appeared on the best seller list. His video *Anyone Can Play the Classic Guitar* (MB95082VX) has become a reference for college students as the authority on basic fundamentals concerning classical technique. He also appears on Mel Bay's videos of the complete volumes of *Modern Guitar Method*, a huge commercial success, selling in the millions of copies.

Bolt divides his time among publishing, performing with orchestras, and teaching at the college level. He believes anyone can play the guitar well, provided they have these three ingredients: a good instrument, a knowledgeable teacher, and music that holds the student's interest.

Bolt's work is distributed internationally and has been featured at the yearly NAMM show (National Association of Music Merchants) in California, as well as the International NAMM show in Germany.

Gardenia Blues
(For Eric Clapton)

Ben Bolt

Movido

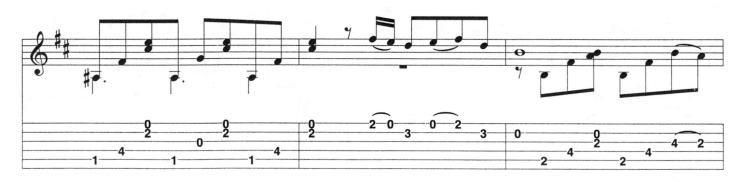

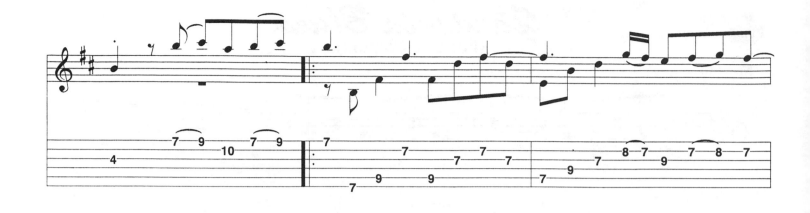

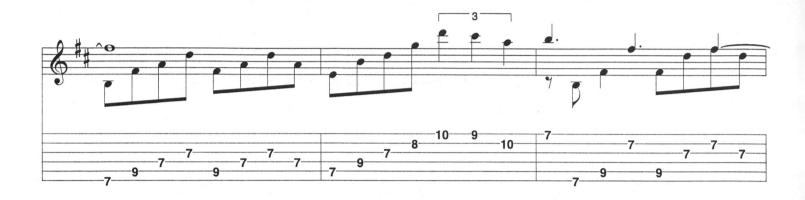

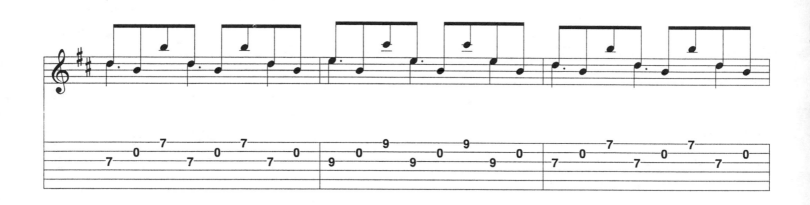

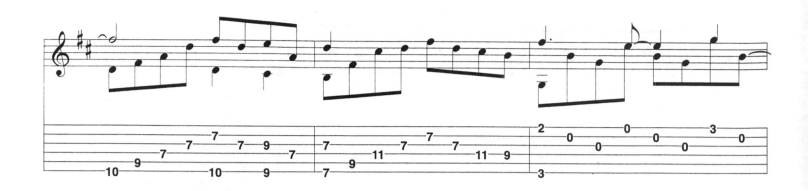

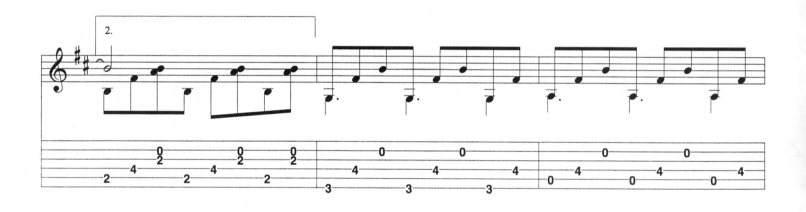

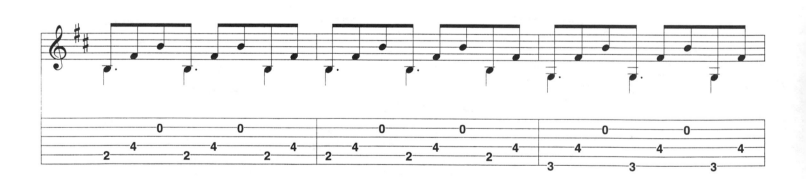

Dan Bowden

*Bowden's trio, **Stingy Brimm**, pictured from left to right:*
Dan Bowden, Geoff Wadsworth and John Walker

Dan Bowden is a guitarist and music educator who resides in Brookline, Massachusetts with his wife and two children. Having graduated from Berklee College of Music in 1980, he joined the Berklee guitar faculty in 1989 teaching blues, jazz, and rock styles. Dan has performed throughout New England and Canada.

Other transcription books available by Dan Bowden are: *Emily Remler Retrospective/Compositions* (MB95579), *Wes Montgomery/The Early Years* (MB95315BCD) *Lightnin' Hopkins/Blues Guitar Legend* (MB95344), and *Mance Lipscomb Texas Blues Guitar Solos* (MB95239).

Rosenannon Blues

Rosenannon is a small village in the southwest county of Cornwall, England where Mel Bay author and Berklee College of Music faculty member Dan Bowden composed this instrumental guitar/harp feature of his acoustic trio; Stingy Brimm. Rosenannon Blues is one of fourteen tracks on the debut Stingy Brimm CD and features Dan on his National Resophonic Style N. Geoff Wadsworth on harmonica and special guest Casey Schuerell on percussion.

Rosenannon Blues

Composed and arranged
by Dan Bowden

Used by Permission

43

45

47

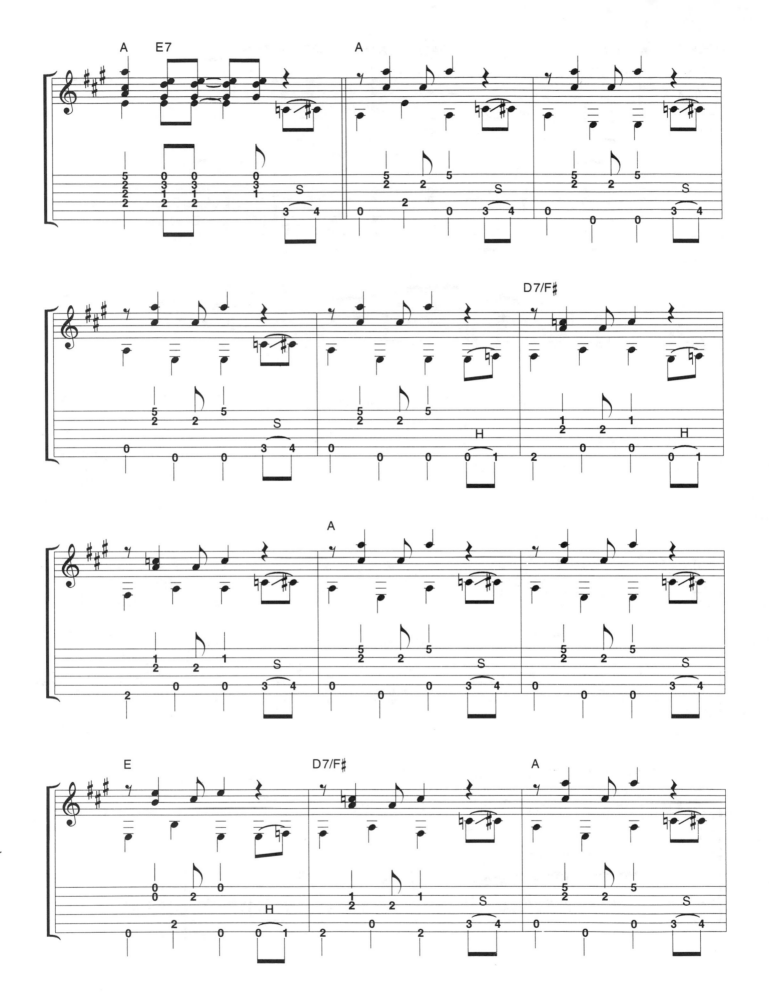

48

50

Dix Bruce

Dix Bruce is a musician and writer from the San Francisco Bay Area. He performs and records with several groups in the San Francisco Bay Area including a guitar duo with Jim Nunally and The Royal Society Jazz Orchestra, a ten-piece big band which performs jazz from the 1920s and 1930s.

To date, Mel Bay publications has published thirty of Bruce's instructional book and CD sets along with two instructional videos. Included are the country guitar and mandolin book/CD sets from the best-selling *You Can Teach Yourself* series along with Bruce's Own *BackUp TRAX* series of play-along rhythm sections, music-minus-one type, book/CD sets for learning everything from bluegrass and old time music, to blues and jazz. In late 1998, he finished a comprehensive book on the early 1960s playing of guitar legend Doc Watson, *Doc Watson & Clarence Ashley, The Original Folkways Recording 1960-1962* (97056). He's currently preparing a book on the playing of Jerry Garcia. Bruce has written for *Acoustic Guitar, FRETS, Bluegrass Unlimited,* and *The Fretted Instrument Guild of America.*

Frogs for Snakes

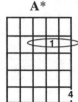

A*

"Frogs For Snakes" is a low down "delta Texas-style" fingerpicked blues. The melody is based on a familiar blues triplet riff, played here with a combination of double stops and bass notes. (If you're not fingerpicking, you can leave out the bass notes and play the melody with a pick.) In measure five (see "") you'll need to use the alternate A chord shown below, which is sometimes referred to as the "hoe handle A."*

Measure 10 has a somewhat unusual chord, the #V ("sharp five") chord (C7). The variation, while rooted in the theme of the melody, demonstrates how you can carry one basic lick through the first eight bars of chord changes. The "i," "m," and "T" designations in the music refer to the picking fingers index, middle, and thumb, respectively. Numbers above the staff are suggested fingerings for your fretting hand.

Frogs for Snakes

by Dix Bruce

From the Mel Bay Publication "BackUP TRAX: Basic Blues Guitar" by Dix Bruce

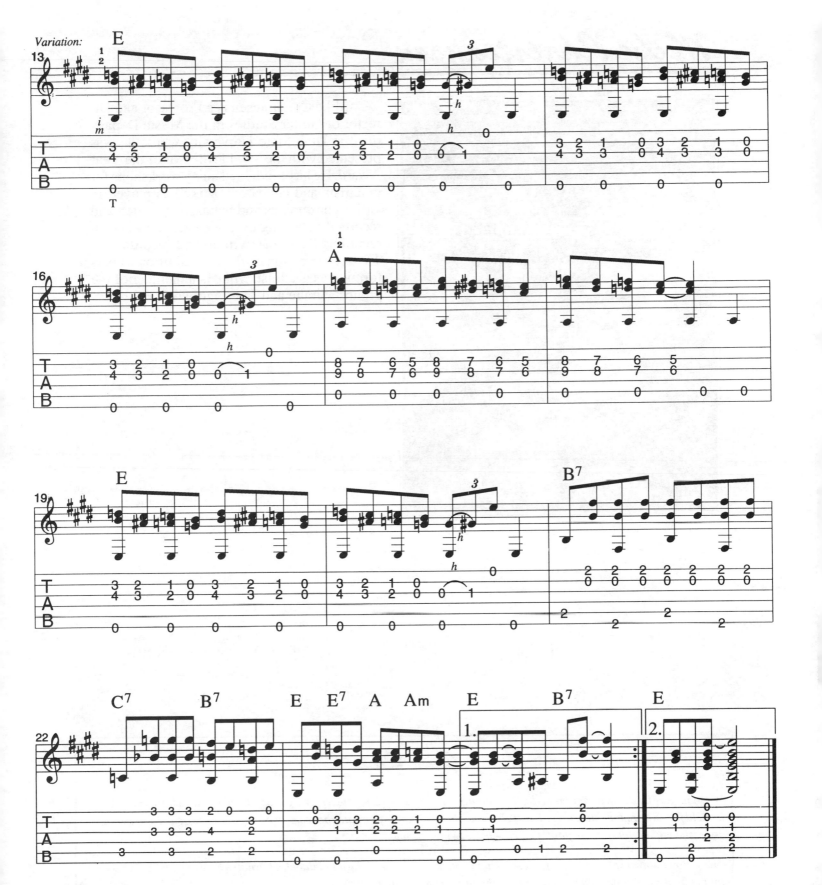

Mike Christiansen

Mike Christiansen is a Professor and Director of Guitar Studies in the Music Department at Utah State University where he was presented with the 1994 Professor of the Year Award. He has conducted many workshops for guitarists and educators. Mike has played in various ensembles and bands, has written and recorded radio jingles, done back-up work on recordings, and has written and recorded for TV and educational films. In addition to performing as a soloist, Mike is a member of the groups Mirage and The Lightwood Duo.

June Rag

When fingerpicking in a ragtime style, the technique is very similar to fingerpicking blues. Generally, a chord form may be held for one or more measures. The right-hand thumb usually alternates between two strings on the beat. In a ragtime style, the eighth notes are usually played with a swing rhythm.

The following two solos are in a fingerpicking ragtime style. The right-hand thumb alternates between two bass notes on the beat. Also, remember to play the eight notes using swing rhythm.

Oscar's Blues

"Oscar's Blues" is a fingerpicking solo which uses the alternating-bass technique. Remember, while playing the notes in each measure, try to hold the chord written above the measure. The chord may have to be modified slightly by lifting a finger, or adding a finger, to play the written notes. Hold as much of the chord as possible.

June Rag

Fingerstyle Solo

Mike Christiansen

Oscar's Blues

Mike Christiansen

Fingerstyle Solo

Ya Da Ya Da

Mike Christiansen

Fingerstyle Solo

♩ = 138

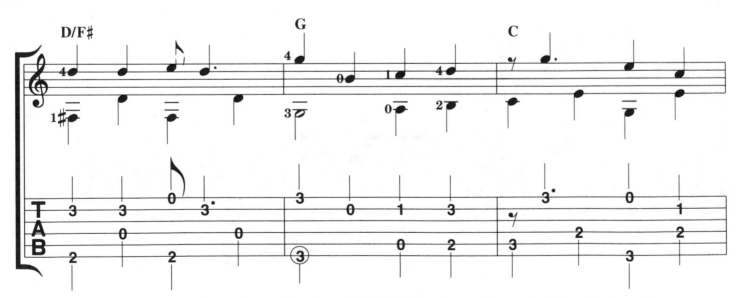

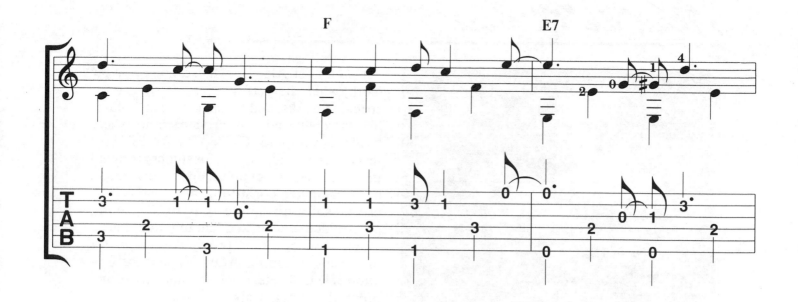

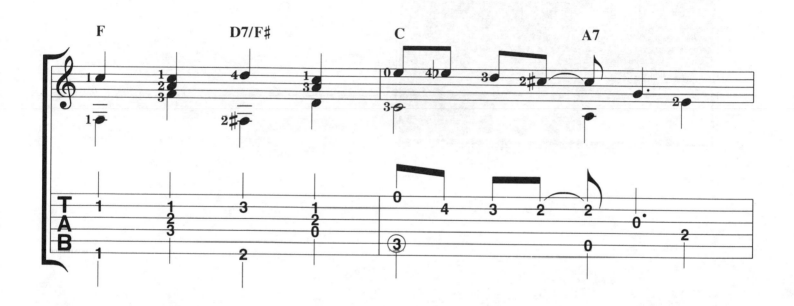

59

Alan de Mause

Guitarist Alan de Mause lives in New York, where he performs, writes music instruction books, and teaches both at Columbia University and at his private studio, where he also develops his GUITAR POWER! correspondence study course for students around the world. When not involved in music, Alan does computer consulting and teaches the use of software applications. Using computer-aided music sequencing and music graphics software, he provides services for musicians including arranging and the creation of lead sheets, flyers, posters, and other promotional materials.

Blues for Phyllis

This blues consists of a theme and two improvised choruses. I intended the whole piece to be reminiscent of electric piano style in the bebop mode: even, flowing eighth notes over sparse comping or single note bass. Notice that the harmony of the second improvised chorus switches from standard blues to an alternate progression. Don't forget to use your rest stroke in the melody to create the punchy nuances of bebop.

Blues for Phyllis

Fingerstyle
medium

You Have Your Basic Bebop Blues

71

Steven Eckels

Guitarist/composer Steven Zdenek Eckels' musical background can be traced to his Czech grandfather, who played violin, and his Swedish grandmother, who played piano and wrote songs. His creative nature springs from growing up making pottery with his father, ceramic artist Robert Eckels.

Steve and his brother Jeff performed as a jazz duo, "The Eckels Brothers," for a number of years before Steve recorded his first solo guitar album in 1981. His creative works now include 15 albums, a vast number of compositions for solo guitar, numerous works for acoustic ensemble, and a congregational liturgy. His "Concerto for Classical Guitar, Jazz Violin and Chamber Orchestra" was premiered by the Lake Superior Chamber Orchestra in 1989.

Steve's education includes a bachelor's degree from Berklee College of Music, Boston, a master's degree from New England Conservatory, education certification from Northland College, Ashland, Wisconsin, and independent study in a variety of areas including ethnomusicology and liturgical music.

He is an author for Mel Bay Publications, Inc., a recording artist for the Whole Person Wellness Corporation, and an award-winning member of the American Society of Composers, Authors, and Publishers (ASCAP). He has been elected to membership in the National Academy of Recording Arts and Sciences.

Steve currently lives in Washburn, Wisconsin with his wife Barbara, where they operate Chequamegon Music, an artist owned, independent record company. He is the guitar instructor for Northland College, an active pastoral musician, and the leader of a dance band, "The Harbor City Roadsters." Still an active potter, his hobbies include hiking and cultivating a wildflower meadow.

Deep River Blues

D.S. ℅ al Coda ⊕

⊕ *Coda*

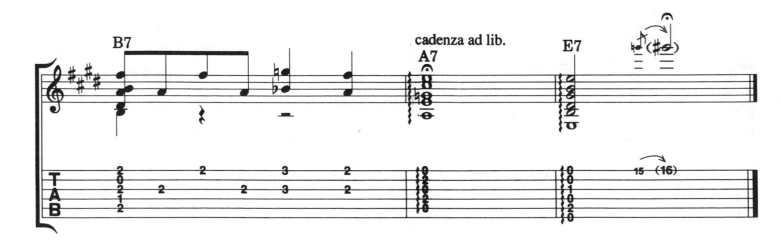

Jim Ferguson

Photo by Brad Shirakawa

In 1994, Jim Ferguson received one of the highest honors of his profession: a Grammy nomination from the National Academy of Recording Arts and Sciences in the Best Album Notes category for annotating Fantasy Records' 12-CD boxed set Wes Montgomery—*The Complete Riverside Recordings,* which includes an incisive biographical essay and interviews with numerous figures, including Nat Adderley, Ron Carter, Kenny Burrell, John Scofield, and Tommy Flanagan. The award marked a recent high point in a career that began in the mid '70s.

For more than 15 years, Ferguson was associated with *Guitar Player Magazine.* A former editor, he specialized in jazz and classical guitar—meeting, interviewing, and writing about virtually every important figure in the guitar world. A specialist in jazz, and in jazz guitar in particular, he contributed the guitar history entry and 14 biographies to *The New Grove Dictionary of Jazz.* He has also annotated over 40 albums (Wes Montgomery, Kenny Burrell, Joe Pass, Jim Hall, Tal Farlow, George Van Eps, Johnny Smith, and many others) and compiled several acclaimed collections of historic performances for the Fantasy, Rhino, and Concord labels. In addition to *Guitar Player*, his hundreds of articles have appeared in *JazzTimes, Down Beat, Classical Guitar, Fingerstyle Guitar,* and other international publications. His books have covered topics ranging from blues to the music of Federico Moreno Torroba.

A noted guitar instructor, Ferguson has a Master of Fine Arts degree from Mills College in Oakland, California, and teaches music at both Evergreen Valley College in San Jose, California, and California State University, Monterey Bay in Seaside, California. He has studied with George Barnes, Red Varner, Lenny Breau, Jose Rey de la Torre, and David Tanenbaum and performed in Europe and the U.S. Moreover, he is profiled in Maurice J. Summerfield's *The Jazz Guitar—Its Evolution, Players And Personalities Since 1900.* Regarding his own approach to jazz, *Cadence Magazine* said, "Bluesy and swinging, Ferguson bears up under repeated listening."

In 1997, Jim founded his own music publishing company, Guitar Master Class, whose first book, *All Blues For Jazz Guitar—Comping Styles, Chords & Grooves* (MB96842BCD), was received virtually with universal acclaim. In 1999, he followed that success with *All Blues Soloing For Jazz Guitar—Scales, Licks, Concepts & Choruses* (98003BCD). Both are distributed by Mel Bay. Busy with future projects, he resides in Santa Cruz, California.

Intro Blues

Jim Ferguson

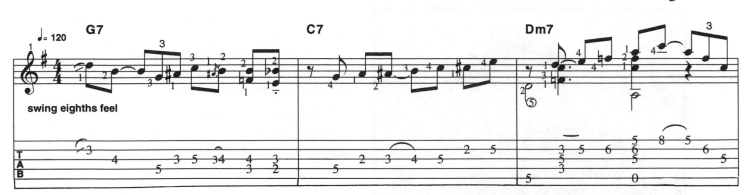
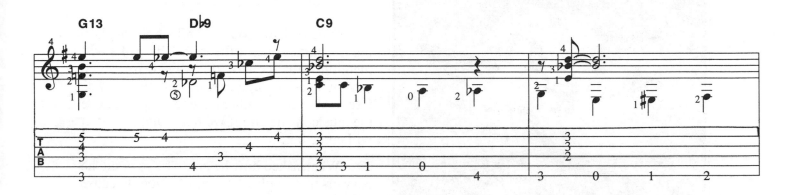
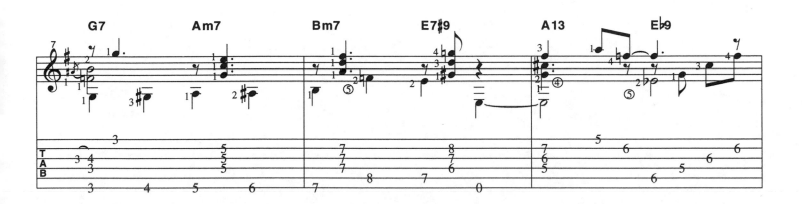

Used by Permission

Buddy Fite

Buddy Fite's guitar style is completely unique in that once you hear him, you can always pick him out. His combination of walking bass line, rhythm and lead at the same time is almost unbelievable.

An interesting note is Buddy's approach to the guitar fingerboard. He approaches it as a keyboard player would, in that he doesn't think in terms of fret position.

* * * * * * * *

When asked about his philosophy at playing the guitar, one of the many things he will mention is that he would always learn which notes wouldn't work in a song first, then he was free to play all the others. He feels we all have the music inside and if we really listen to it, it will come out.

When asked how he got to be so good, he answers that he plays the way he does because nobody ever told him he couldn't.

-Denny Handa

Blues for Amos Johnson

Tommy Flint

John Griggs

Since founding the Griggs School of Music in Norfolk, Virginia in 1957, John Griggs has taught thousands of pupils to play jazz and classical guitar. Many of his pupils have become teachers and world-class performers in their own right. Mr. Griggs was a guitar instructor for 20 years at Old Dominion University. He continues to teach privately, but devotes most of his energies to performing and transcribing, arranging, and composing for the guitar.

Try Me Blues

Edited by Charlie Byrd

By John Griggs
(BMI)

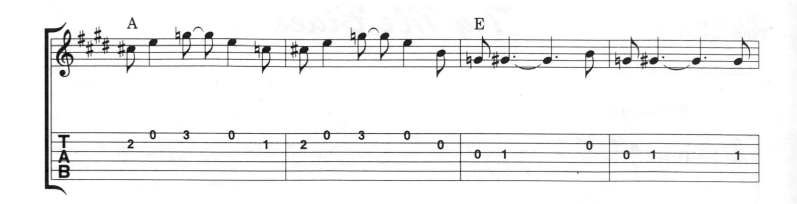

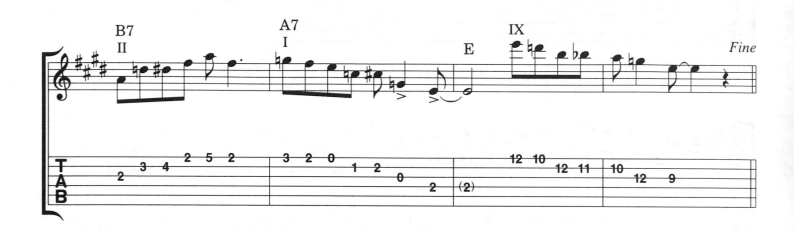

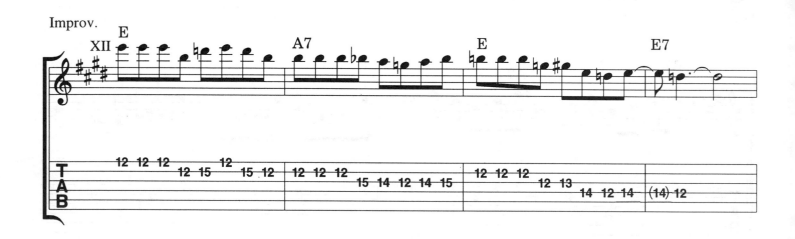

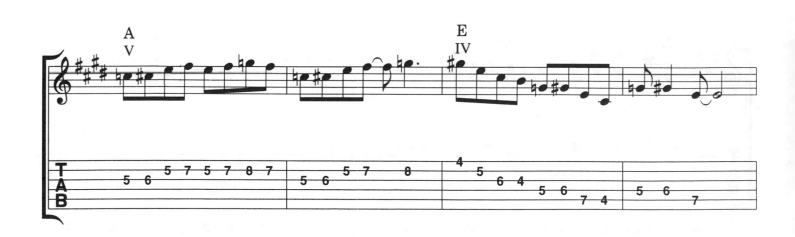

104

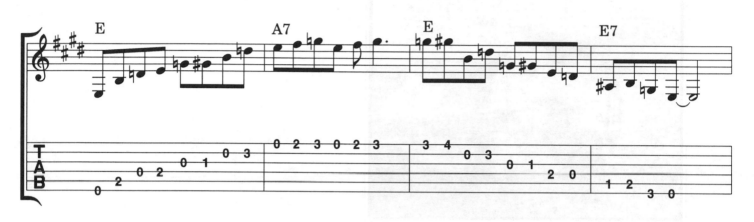

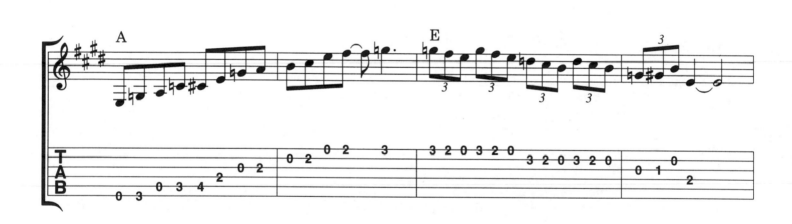

Stefan Grossman

Stefan Grossman has been recording, performing, and writing about acoustic fingerstyle techniques and styles for more than 30 years. During the period from 1965-1975 he studied and traveled with some of the legendary figures in the world of blues guitar. From the period came his landmark five-volume series for Oak Publications. Stefan has written many other books that have been published by Mel Bay Publications. Stefan has also recorded numerous solo albums for Shanachie Records.

A Heart Much Obliged

Swing (♩♩ = ♩♩)

Stefan Grossman

108

109

Ole Halén

Ole Anders Halén began studying electric guitar at age 13. By the time he was 15, he found himself in a touring rock band with several hit records. He was subsequently influenced by the playing style of Chet Atkins and at 17, in order to improve his fingerstyle technique, he began to study the classical guitar. On the recommendation of his teacher, Ivan Putilin, Halén studied classical music at the Sibelius Academy in Helsinki, Finland where he was later to occupy a guitar teaching position himself.

Blues for Paavo

Ole Halen

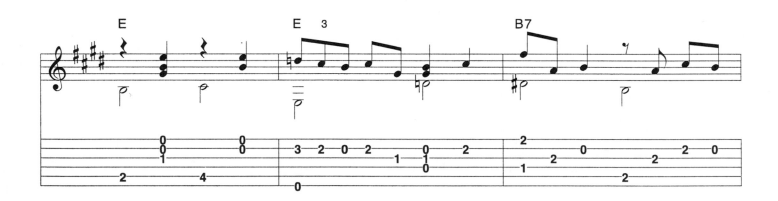

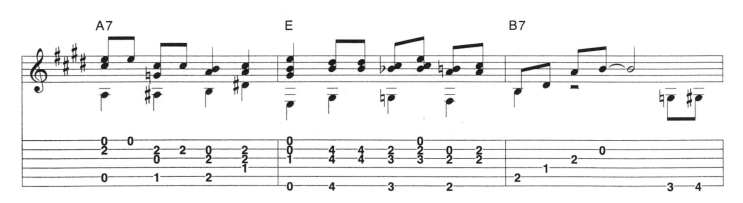

Used by Permission

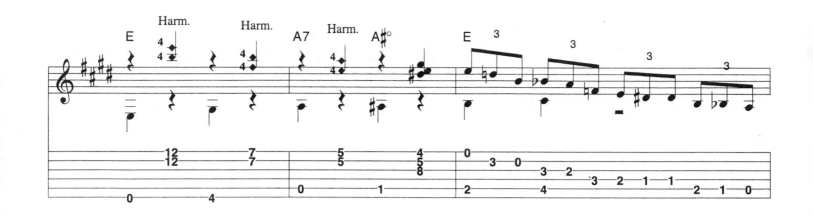

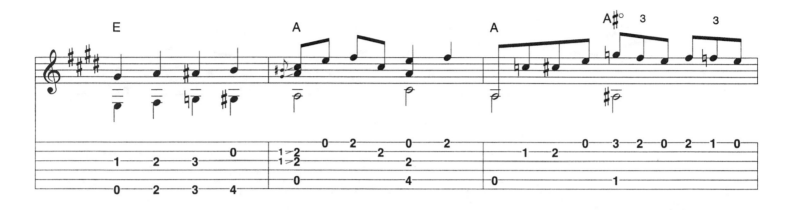

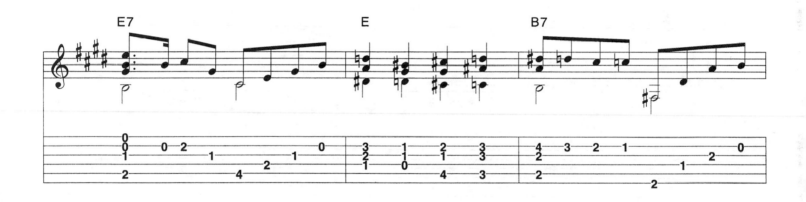

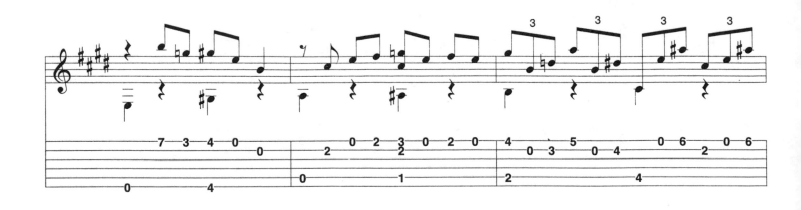

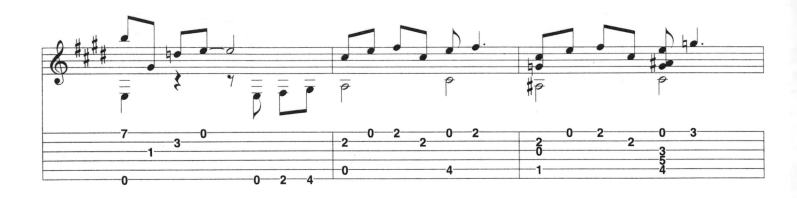

Al Hendrickson

Al Hendrickson was born in Eastland, Texas. He became recognized as a premier jazz guitarist during stints with the Artie Shaw band and the famed Gramercy Five. Al later played with the Benny Goodman band and sextet. Known for his outstanding rhythm and chord playing, he became much sought after by leading band leaders. Al performed with Woody Herman, Johnny Mandel, Dizzy Gillespie, Louis Bellson, Ray Noble and Neal Hefti among others. Al settled in Los Angeles and became one of the busiest studio guitarists in America. He estimates that he played on over 5000 film soundtracks from 1939 to 1980! In addition, Al backed such notable musicians and singers as Frank Sinatra, Peggy Lee, Nat "King" Cole, Benny Carter, and Lena Horne. He played in orchestras led by Lalo Schifrin, Nelson Riddle and Quincy Jones.

Blues Lite

Al Hendrickson 93

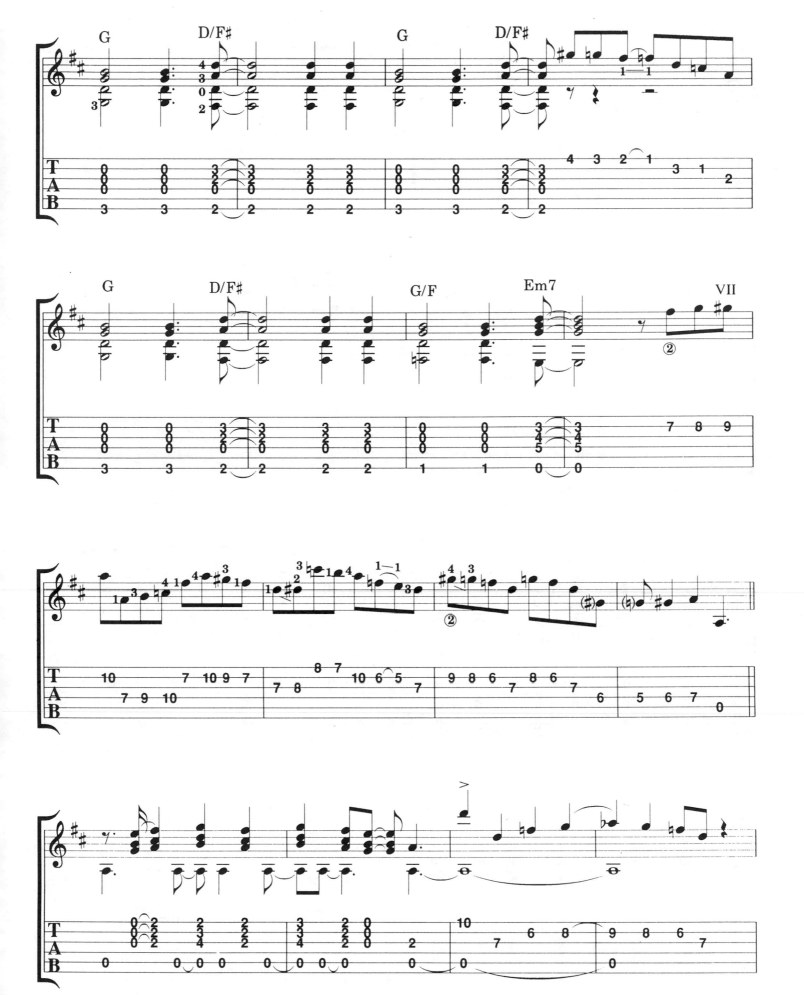

117

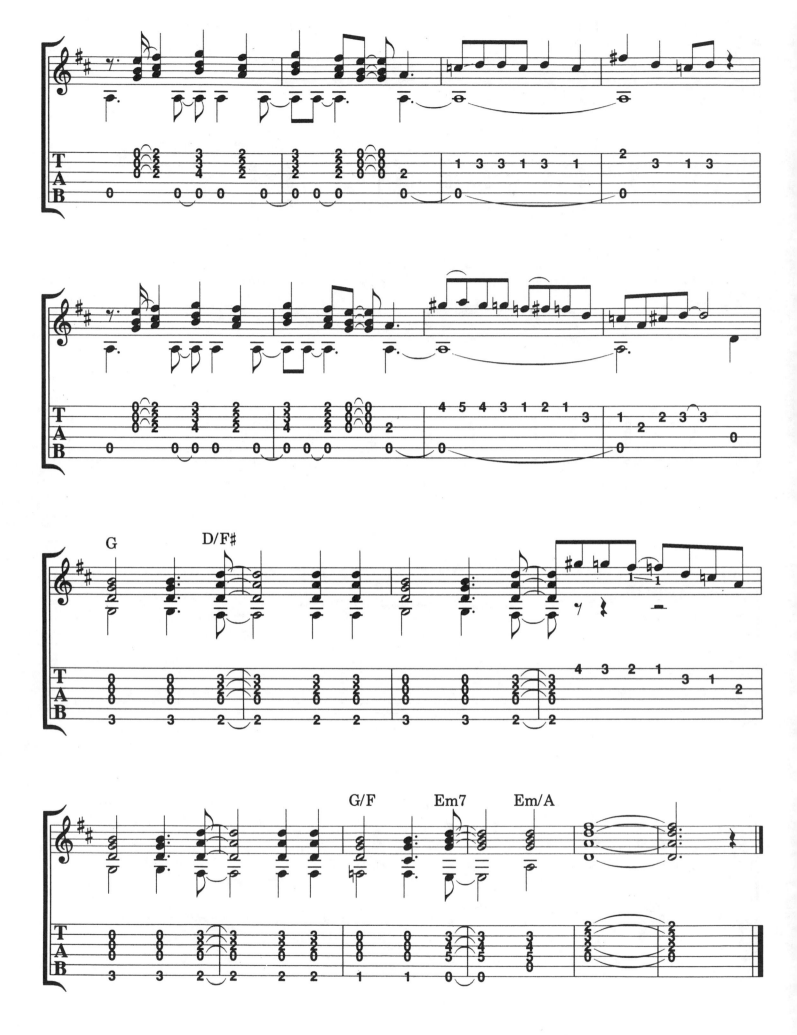

118

*This page has been
left blank to avoid
awkward page turns*

Roger Hudson

Born in 1961, Roger Hudson represents a new breed of classically-trained composer/ guitarist. Hudson's approach is in the spirit of composers for the guitar such as Augustine Barrios-Mangore, Fernando Sor, Mauro Giuliani, Francisco Tárrega and Leo Brouwer. All of these artists wrote as skilled composers but also as guitarists. So it is unique music that is enjoyed by guitarists and the general audience alike. The Guitar Foundation of America's journal Soundboard spoke of "...many gorgeous moments..." and "strong themes" in describing Hudson's compositions.

Hudson began playing the guitar at age 12 in the Virginia suburbs of Washington, D.C. and learned the variety of musical styles that he draws upon in his works. He has studied guitar with John Sutherland, Christopher Berg, Fred Sabback, and in master classes with Christopher Parkening. Hudson studied composition with Charles Knox and Tayloe Harding at Georgia State University where he earned a master's degree in music theory. He maintains a busy schedule of concerts, television and radio appearances, recording, composing, and teaching as well as being on the teaching staff at MARS Nashville. He currently resides in Nashville, Tennessee with his wife Brenda and two children, Camille and Elijah.

Blue Stairway

Walking with Swing

Roger Hudson

Jean-Felix Lalanne

Jean-Felix Lalanne discovered the guitar at age twelve. Playing by ear, he spent many hours each day practicing. This, coupled with his innate musical ability, earned him his first solo concert only one year later. At fourteen he entered the Academy of Guitar in Marseilles, France where he studied classical guitar and orchestration.

In 1978, at 16 years of age, Jean-Felix won the prestigious French National Contest of Classical Guitar which presented him with credentials allowing him to study guitar anywhere in the world. The following year Jean-Felix moved to Paris where he began touring extensively, recorded his first solo album and became a much sought-after studio musician.

Acting as producer and arranger, Jean-Felix has recently completed the latest CD for French pop artist "Patsy" and is working on a new duet album with American guitarist Muriel Anderson.

Sweet Sadness

G♯m looks like an unfamiliar key for the guitar and yet it sounds so good. This is one of Jean-Felix's favorites.

Again some far-reaching positions, measures 18 and 19, where you may move your hand without making any other note ring.

At measure 21 are many chords in a row. Work this out carefully.

The [B] part illustrates Jean Felix's way to play rhythm. He got the idea by listening to how drummers give that jazzy triplet impulse. The first two notes of the triplets are muted. Play the triplet **p i p**.

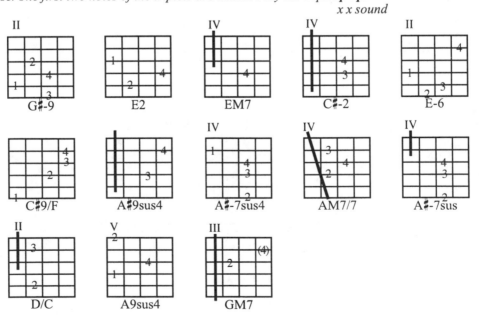

122

Sweet Sadness

Jean-Félix LALANNE

125

Paul Lolax

Photo by Johanna Lolax

Paul Lolax is a Vermont-based musician and music instructor. He is a Stowe resident who has played guitar for more than 30 years.

His career as a performer began in 1967 in Boston, Massachusetts, where he played solo and backup guitar at various coffeehouses and restaurants. *Broadside Magazine* voted him "Best Instrumentalist of the Year" in 1968. During the early '70s he toured the national college circuit, did studio work in Baltimore, Maryland, played in social service settings such as Boston's Charles Street Jail, and served as an artist-in-residence at independent schools in Massachusetts.

He has played with two groups and as a soloist in numerous home, church, wedding, restaurant, and social service settings since relocating to Vermont seven years ago. He also has appeared on the cable access program Vermont Folk Stage.

Paul was born in New York City and raised in Worchester, Massachusetts. He has written for *Acoustic Guitar* magazine, and wrote the book *Transcriptions of Scott Joplin and Joseph Lamb* (Hansen House). He recorded *Selected Works of Scott Joplin and Joseph Lamb* (Titanic Records). He studied classical guitar with Aaron Shearer at the Peabody Conservatory in Baltimore, and has played bass guitar and the mandolin in addition to acoustic guitar.

JoBlues

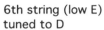
Paul Lolax

6th string (low E)
tuned to D

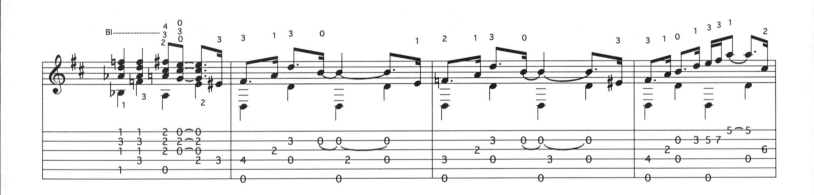

To Coda ⊕

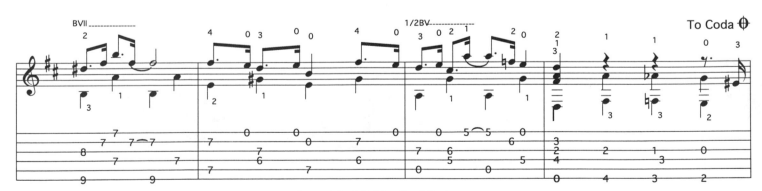

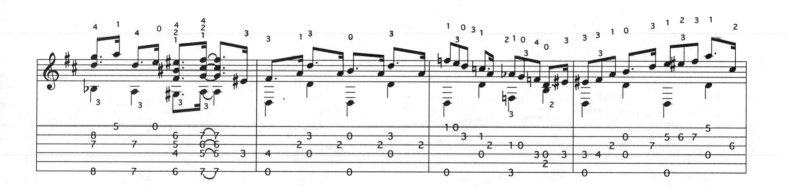

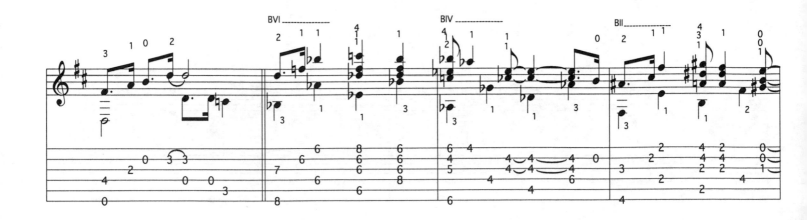

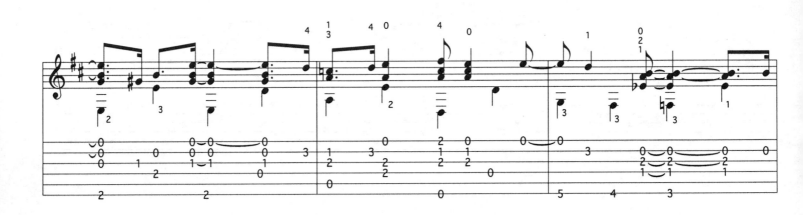

Larry McCabe

Photo by Karl Rehbaum

Born in Kansas City, Missouri, Larry studied music with a number of teachers including Eldon Shamblin, legendary swing guitarist and arranger for Bob Wills. Deciding of freelance teaching as a music career, Larry received his degree in Education from the University of Arizona in 1979.

Since graduating from college, Larry has taught over 30,000 private music lessons. He has also taught music history with a focus on American popular music and jazz. An experienced blues guitarist, he played in the Gulf Coast Blues Band, wrote a *Living Blues* magazine column called "Blues Box," and is currently on the nominating committee for the annual W.C. Handy awards. He also enjoys playing Irish fiddle music.

Larry's vast experience in private lessons has given him a unique understanding of the educational needs of the typical music student. Beginning with *Blues, Boogie and Rock Guitar* (93996BCD) in 1984, he has written a number of Mel Bay books on various subjects including guitar, bass, and song writing techniques.

Eight Hour Shift

Performed by the Heat-Seeking Missile Blues Band of Tallahassee, Florida
Charles Atkins, *Vocal* • Randy Barnhill, *Bass* • Marc Blair, *Drum* • Larry McCabe, *Guitar* • Engineer: Fred Chester

Blues music was conceived by a merging of Negro spirituals, work songs, and traditional folk songs. In turn, blues itself has influenced a number of other styles, including jazz, R&B, rockabilly, rock and roll, country, Zydeco, and contemporary gospel. It is very important for a musician to listen to both the musical antecedents of the blues and the later styles that were influenced by the blues. To the musician, listening is nourishment for the musical imagination.

All too often, blues guitarists acquire a one-dimensional style that relies excessively on the minor pentatonic scale. Furthermore, there is often an overdose of string-bending, which can become tiresome after a while. Happily, such limitations can easily be cured by listening to a variety of music, learning a few new scales, and developing a solid alternate-picking technique. When these things are done, a musician will truly be able to create many shades of blue in his blues playing.

Performance notes for the solo in "Eight Hour Shift"

• The solo is played to a basic 12-bar "urban blues" progression in the key of G.

• There is no string bending in this solo.

• Rhythmically, the solo is mostly based on triplets.

• The pickup notes climb up the G minor pentatonic scale from G to F. All the notes are played on the third string. The G minor **pentatonic scale** contains the notes G Bb C D F G. Observe the fingering carefully (see the music staff), even if you are working from the tablature.

• The descending lick in mes. 1 is mostly in the **G mixolydian scale**: G A B C D E F G.

• The lick in measure 2 is mostly in the **C lydian dominant scale**: C D E F# G A Bb C.

• Measures 3-4 are based on the **G blues scale** (this is a minor pentatonic scale with an added raised fourth tone). The G blues scale contains the notes G Bb C C# D F G.

• The Chuck Berry-style lick in measures 5-6 is in the **C mixolydian scale**: C D E F G A Bb C.

• In measure 7, the syncopated double-stop lick is harmonized in thirds taken from G mixolydian. "Pinch" each doublestop as follows: play the lower note with a downpick; play the upper note with an up-motion of the middle fingernail.

• The first part of measure 8 uses a popular blues lick based on Jimmy Smith's "Chicken Shack" riff.

• Your alternate-picking skills will be tested with the lick in measure 9. "Pinch" the split-string doublestop at the end of the measure.

• Measure 10 shows how to use the open E string against the C7 chord. The tritone lick (E to Bb) at the end of the measure is a favorite of Clarence "Gatemouth" Brown.

• The notes in measure 11, played over G7, could also be played over a measure of G7 / C7 /.

• The solo ends much like it started, with the pickup notes played on a different string.

• The fill-ins in this solo appear in **Mel Bay's 101 Dynamite Blues Guitar Fill-In Licks** (97014BCD).

Eight Hour Shift

Solo

Larry McCabe

If you enjoy jazz-blues guitar and swing guitar, see the following Mel Bay book/CD sets by Larry McCabe:

101 Red Hot Swing Guitar Licks (97335BCD)
101 Red Hot Jazz-Blues Guitar Licks and Solos (98338BCD)
101 Dynamite Blues Guitar Fill-In Licks (97014BCD)
Blues Band Rhythm Guitar (94825BCD)

Dale Miller

Dale Miller is a fingerstyle guitarist living in Berkeley, California with his wife and two cats. He spends his time writing feature and instructional articles for *Acoustic Guitar Magazine*, teaching private guitar lessons, playing the occasional gig, serving as a computer consultant and trouble shooter for a San Francisco law firm and working at *Noe Valley Music*, the San Francisco guitar shop he co-owns. Mel Bay Publications has also released another book/CD package by Miller entitled *Dale Miller/Country Blues & Ragtime Guitar Styles* (96557BCD).

Dale's Boogie Blues

The feel of this tune is reminiscent of the playing of Texas blues stylist and songster Mance Lipscomb, who was a major influence of mine as I discussed in the intro to the last tune. Lipscomb was the same age as folks like Mississippi John Hurt, Skip James, and Bukka White but had no professional career in the 1920s and 1930s. He lived as a share cropper in Navasota, Texas until his discovery by Chris Strachqitz of Arhoolie Records in the 1960s. He was a professional musician for the last ten years of his life, and no early bluesman played better or put on a more impressive show. With no evidence to the contrary, it's comforting for middle-aged guitarists like myself to think that Lipscomb slowly improved his whole life and played his best music in his sixties and seventies.

Notice how adding the different bass note at the end of the measures in A to an otherwise monotonic bass line creates a bit of interest and drive. This note not only complicates the bass line but becomes part of the melody line as well. "The John Hurt Riff" uses the same bass line in a different key and tuning.

The turnaround is from the playing of *Robert Johnson and is one I use all the time for blues in this key. On a slow blues I'll give it a more triplet feel. On the recurring slide lick move up the entire 2/3* D9th *barre A chord and have the pinky ready to get that high A note. For the D9, I use the following simple fingering with my thumb wrapped over teh back of the neck to get the low F♯.*

The variations are played with the index finger playing a 2/3 barre on the second fret. These licks are easier to play and work even better in the key of G, by the way, with the nut taking the place of the barre.

I decided to capo at the fourth fret on this tune for a brighter sound.

Tampa Red

Born Hudson Woodbridge in Smithvile, Georgia in 1903, Red became a studio musician in Atlanta and Chicago. He was very light skinned and had red hair. He played slide in open E style tuning and often dueted with pianist Thomas A. "Georgia Tom" Dorsey, who became one of gospel music's biggest stars. Red's style was more melodic than chordal, and he really exploited the sustain and fat tone of his National guitar.

The first time through this composition while in the tonic E chord I play a boogie-woogie bass line under mostly   *arpeggiated open-string licks in the treble. This technique is not from Red, but I worked it out after learning his "Boogie Woogie Dance" as a contrast to the fat ringing licks he uses. These licks have become the variation or "break" in this tune. In this tuning the IV (A) and V7 (B7) chords are gingered like this.*

If you like to sing try out a rock 'n' roll or jump blues chestnut like "Whole Lot a Shakin' Goin' On" or "Shake, Rattle and Roll" with the boogie-woogie bass section.

Other traditional slide players who used this tuning include Blind Willie Johnson and Robert Johnson.

CD #2
Track #2

Dale's Boogie Blues

Capo IV—true key is C♯   Dale Miller

Tampa Red

E tuning = E B E G♯ B E

Dale Miller

Franco Morone

With a repertoire ranging from blues and Celtic tunes to jazz, Italian fingerstylist Franco Morone is recognized as one of the most gifted performers on the international guitar scene. Adhering to the concept of the "folk process" in which traditional music, while retaining its roots, evolves continually to remain fresh and current - Franco transforms diverse elements of folk music incorporating contemporary impressions. Through this process, his arrangements of traditional Irish and Italian folk melodies acquire a radically new and original quality.

Respected for the excellence and diversity of his work, Franco artfully blends echoes of the past with a variety of contemporary influences in his original compositions. His live performances can be quiet and reserved, or rousing and impetuous-but always mature and highly personalized. Franco regularly participates in international music festivals and frequently tours Europe, the U.S., and Japan in addition to maintaining a rigorous teaching schedule of private students, workshops, and magazine columns.

Fat Boy Blues

I discovered the open-C tuning (low to high: CGCGCE) through American guitarists like Leo Kottke and John Fahey. The sound of open-C tuning is reminiscent of a crude blues-rock sound, and I like to use this tune to open my live sets. The tune is included on a CD called Guitàrea; released by Acoustic Music Records in Osnabrück, Germany.

The rest in the bass line often coincide with a percussive blow by the right-hand thumb. The double percussion figure in measures 1 and 2 is played first by the index of the left hand followed immediately by the thumb of the right-hand. Please listen to the companion CD for a guide to the use of this technique.

*Notes with down-stems are played by the right-hand thumb, except for the notes marked "i" which indicates they are to be played by the index finger of the right hand. Notes with up-stems are played by other fingers of the right hand. **B** and **R** indicate bend and release respectively.*

138

Fat Boy Blues

Tuning : CGCGCE

Franco Morone

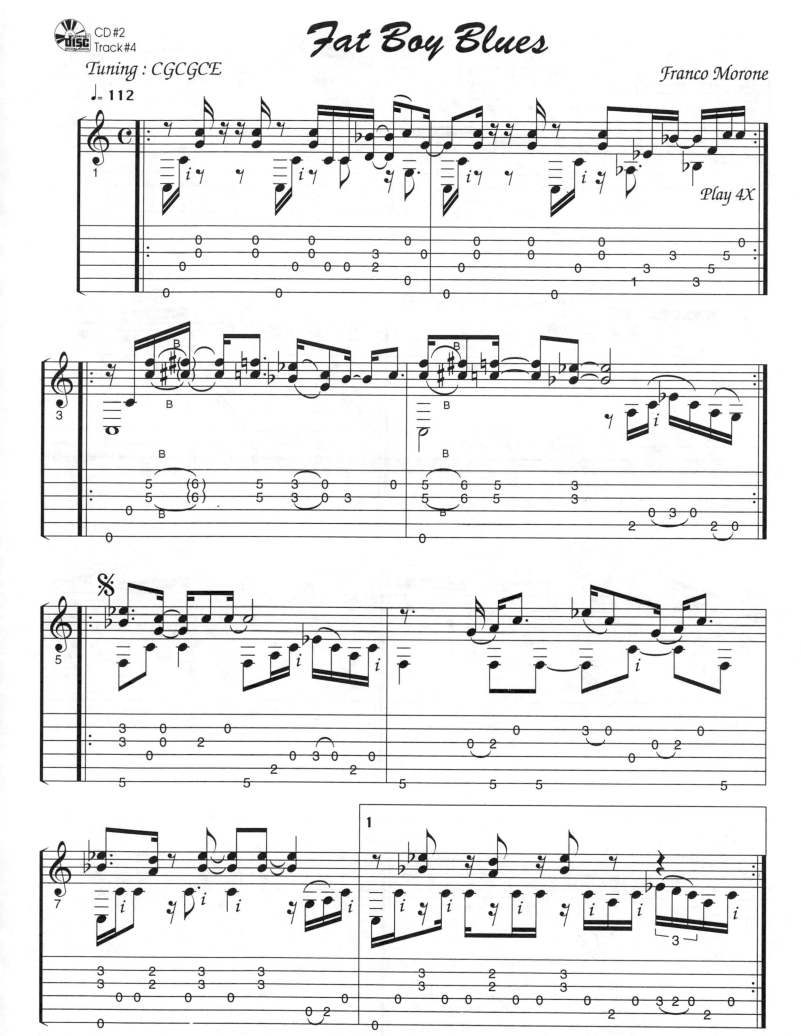

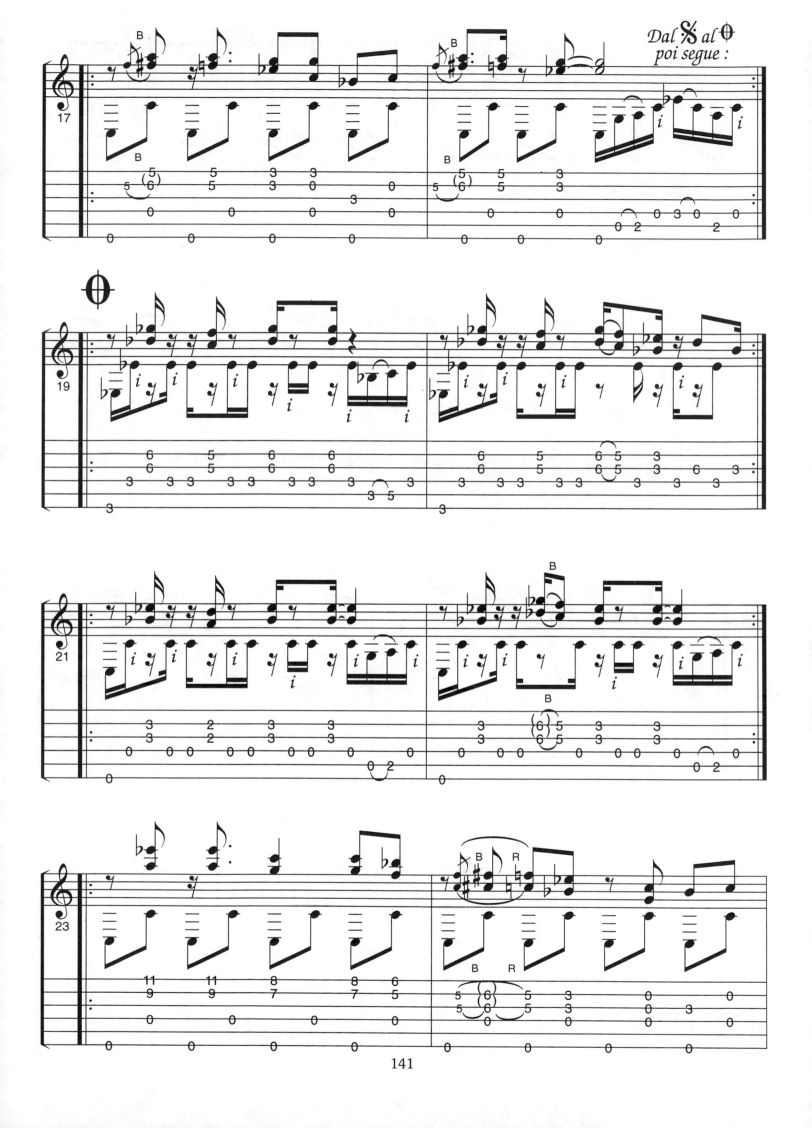

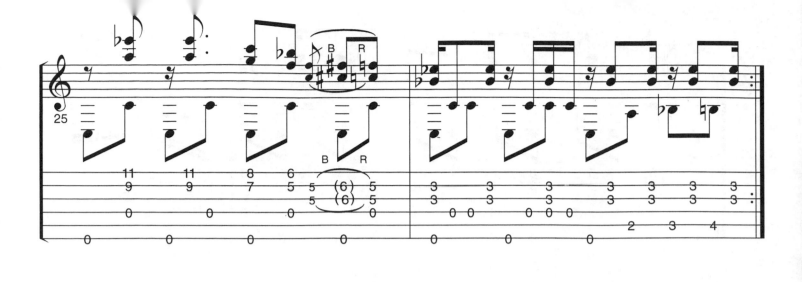

Ronald Muldrow

Born in swinging Chicago, Ronald Muldrow's first vivid experience of live music came at a very early age. Ronald remembers, "My mother took me along to the show at the Regal theater. I was very excited because I had never seen music played live. The band that opened the show played Three Blind Mice as their first tune. I didn't understand what they were playing, but I knew that tune. Their shiny horns under the colored lights made it all the more a magical experience. Later I learned that the band I heard was Art Blakey's Jazz Messengers."

During a hospital stay in his teens, he heard Wes Montgomery playing Canadian Sunset on the radio. "I hadn't been listening to jazz up to that point; I would not have a clue as to what instrument Wes was playing if the DJ had not announced that was Wes Montgomery on guitar." Ronald's subsequent influences on guitar include Kenny Burrell, Grant Green, and Phil Upchurch.

Down Bay the Bijou

RONALD MULDROW

Used by Permission

144

Paul Musso

Mr. Musso is a versatile guitarist, trained in jazz, blues, classical and Latin styles. Paul performs throughout the Colorado area in many diverse musical settings including jazz festivals, symphonic work, musical theater and live music venues. Paul currently teaches guitar studies at the University of Colorado at Denver College of Music, where he has taught for the past seven years. He also teaches guitar, music theory and music history at the Community College of Denver School of Music.

Bird Blues

Jazz Blues

Bill Piburn

Bill Piburn is a native of Kansas City, Missouri and now resides in Nashville, Tennessee. He studied classical guitar with Douglas Niedl and Christopher Parkening and studied jazz with pianist John Elliott. His transcriptions have appeared in *Acoustic Guitar Magazine* and he has been a columnist for *Fingerstyle Guitar* and *Just Jazz Guitar* magazines. He is the author of *Mel Bay's Complete Book of Fiddle Tunes for Acoustic Guitar* (95471).

Bill's playing and arranging have won him praise from guitarists such as Martin Taylor, Charlie Byrd, Jorge Morel, Chet Atkins and Jack Wilkins.

Frankie & Johnny

Arranged by
Bill Piburn

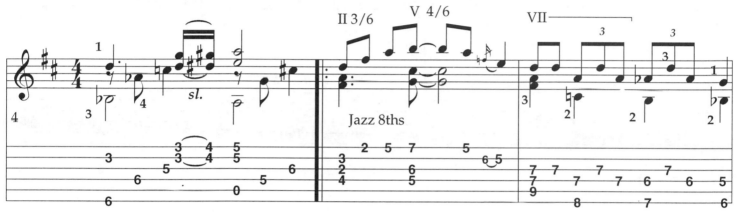

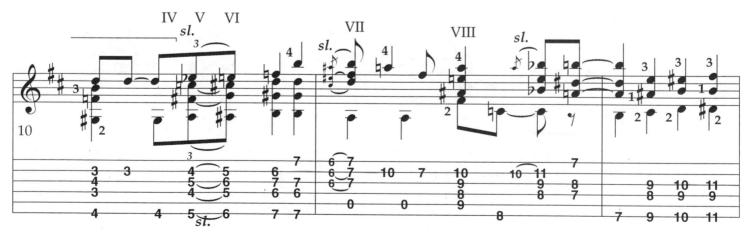

Used by Permission

153

154

155

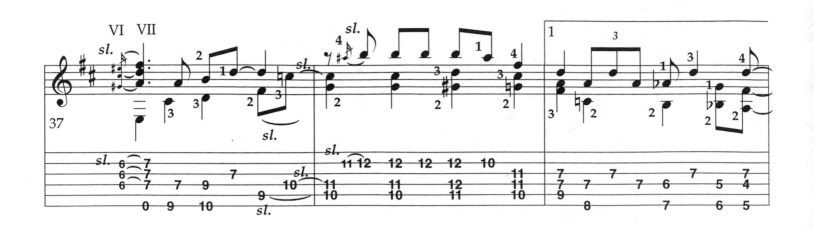

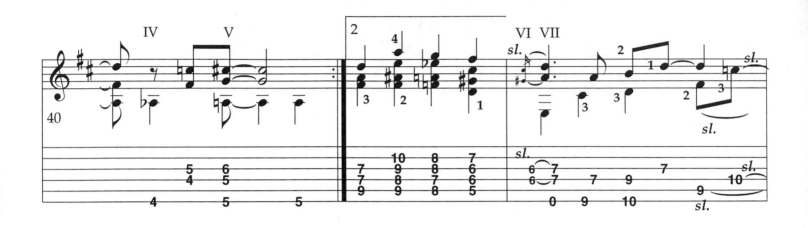

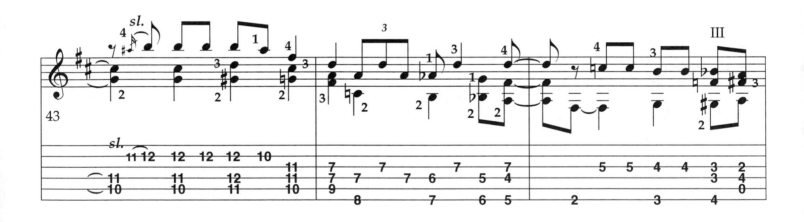

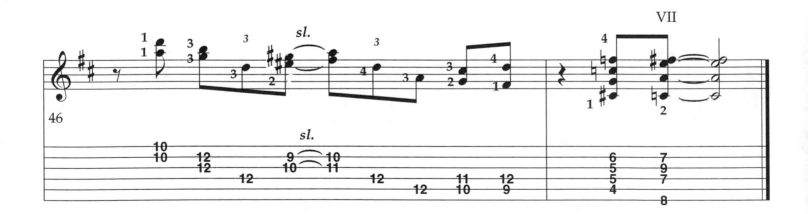

John "Bucky" Pizzarelli

John "Bucky" Pizzarelli is an internationally renowned man of music. His instrument of choice is the guitar, and his style is jazz. For more that half a century, "Bucky," as he is affectionately known, has been a part of the fraternity of musicians who have kept mainstream and traditional jazz alive. The list of big bands and vocalists with whom Bucky has performed and recorded reads like a veritable *Who's Who of Jazz*. He joined Vaughn Monroe's band while still in high school and later played with studio bands at the major networks. There he distinguished himself as one of the best rhythm guitarists in the business. Not contended with studio work alone, he jammed with and accompanied the best in the pop and jazz world including George Barnes, Stéphane Grappellli, Slam Steward, Zoot Sims, Flip Phillips, and his sons Martin and John Pizzarelli. Dedicated to swing and American popular song, Bucky is one of the most sought after guitarists in the business, and at a spry 72 years old, continues to enchant audiences worldwide.

Over and Over Blues

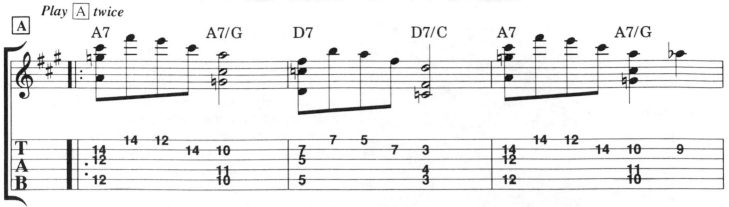

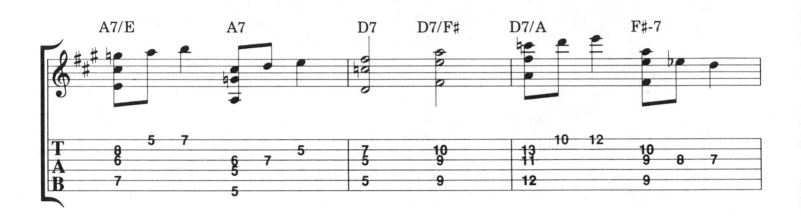

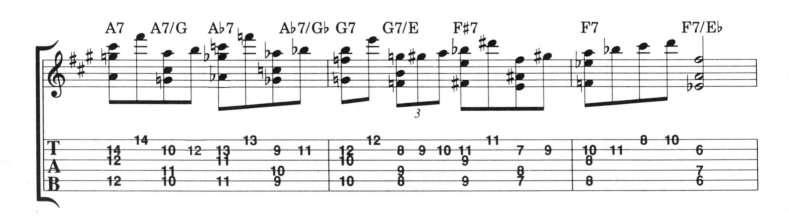

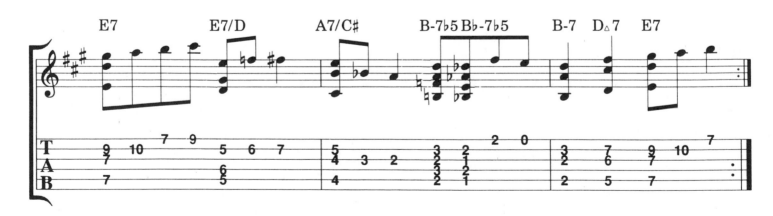

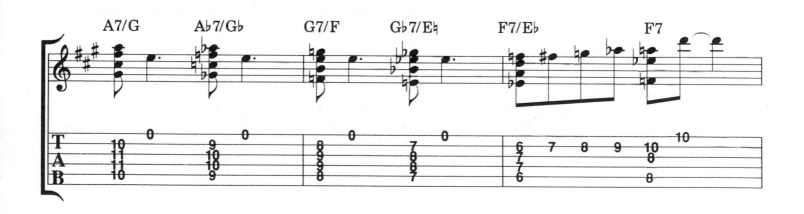

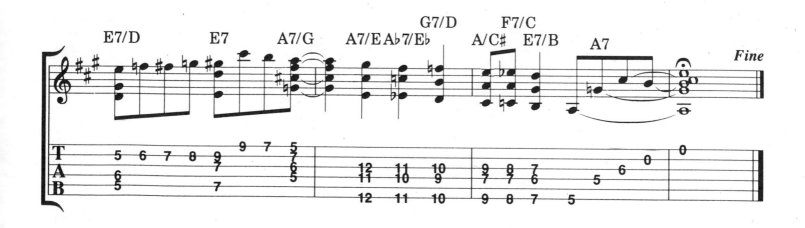

159

Paul Rishell

Photo by Eric H. Antoniou

Paul Rishell was born January 17, 1950 in Brooklyn, New York.

His early musical experience was a drummer playing rock 'n' roll and surf music in Connecticut in the early 1960s. In 1963 a friend introduced him to the country blues recordings of Son House and Robert Johnson, Charlie Patton and Blind Lemon Jefferson. By 1970 he was proficient on both acoustic and electric guitar and worked as a sideman and studio player in Boston. He played with Son House, Johnny Shines, Sonny Terry and Brownie McGhee, and Howlin' Wolf, and shared the stage with many of his blues heroes. In 1975, Paul began performing regularly as a solo acoustic blues artist, and also attracted a strong local following with his own blues band. *Blues For Tampa Red* first appeared on Paul's third album for Tone-Cool records, *I Want You To Know*, in 1996. It features the harmonica work of partner Annie Raines, who can be heard on that album and their 1999 release, *Moving To The Country*. A steadfast touring and recording team, they have been gaining an ever greater following in the U.S. and overseas, performing and teaching at festivals, workshops, clubs and concert halls. Paul plays and endorses National Reso-phonic guitars.

Blues for Tampa Red

♩=180

Paul Rishell

Tuning: E B E G♯ B E

162

164

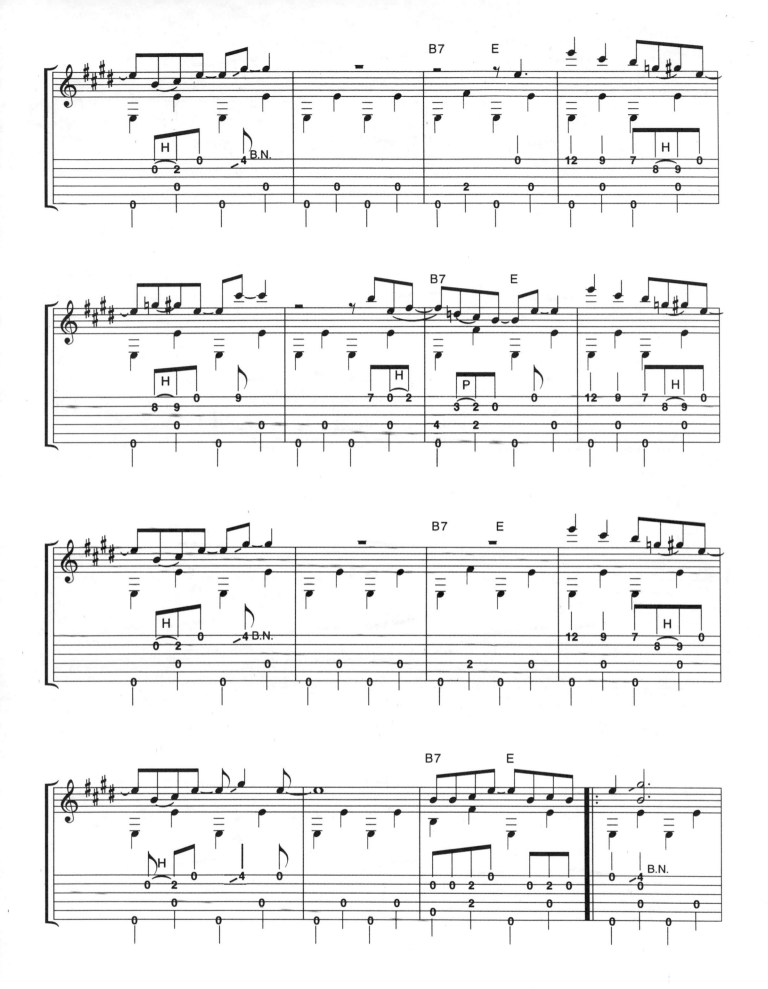

165

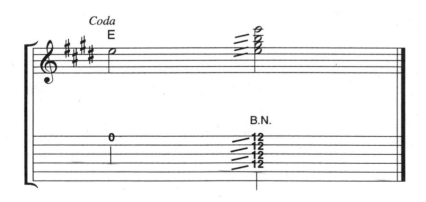

Vincent Sadovsky

Vincent Sadovsky is no stranger to the music industry. In 1973 he opened an acoustic music store in Rochester, Michigan which he and his wife still operate.

He has been teaching guitar, banjo, mountain dulcimer and autoharp since 1970, and has become one of the most sought after instructors in Michigan for composition and technical ability.

Over the years, Vincent has appeared on television and radio broadcasts. His performing has taken him from coffeehouses to festivals, to performing for dignitaries including former president, George Bush. His expertise allowed him to become an "Artist In Residence" for the Michigan Council For The Arts. His passion for acoustic music led him to found and establish the Paint Creek Folklore Society, a nationally known society of acoustic musicians which has been active since 1973. Vincent's playing has appeared on radio and television commercials, documentary films and as a studio musician on various recordings.

Since 1976, Vincent has won numerous banjo competitions, and is known for his use of the "Keith" tuners. His landmark publication, *New Twists For The Five String Banjo* sells worldwide.

As a result of Vincent's continued fascination with the "Keith" tuners, he has put his banjo aside and developed his technique for the guitar. The use of the "Keith" tuners along with his solid fingerstyle adds a new dimension to the art of guitar playing.

"I first heard Vince Sadovsky play over fifteen years ago, and even then his music was remarkable. The banjo was his main instrument at the time, and he was writing music using the special tuners I had developed with my partner, Dan Bump. Now he is applying his playing and writing skills (and the tuners) to the guitar, and is composing some of the finest original pieces that I've heard, tunes that are new and unique but that seem like old friends. And after you hear Vince play, I bet you'll find yourself humming these tunes too." - Bill Keith

Chicago Joe

Vincent Sadovsky

Swing

To ⊕ Coda

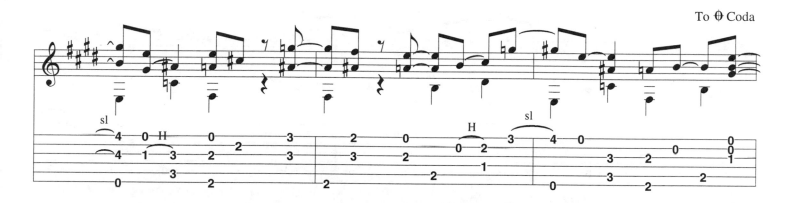

D.S. al Coda

⊕ CODA

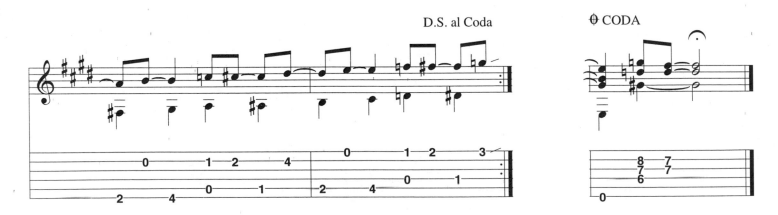

Felix Schell

Felix Schell was born June 25, 1951 in Mainz/Germany. At age 13, Felix began teaching himself the guitar (mostly using songs of the Beatles and the Rolling Stones). Later, he began to study jazz guitar, harmony and theory at the Jazz School Munique. Two years later, Felix became a teacher for the school.

Throughout the years, Felix played in several bands from R & R to jazz and toured with the musical "Hair" for some time. He also wrote big band arrangements and several instruction books for the guitar.

Emma

OPEN G-TUNING:
DGDGHD

Felix Schell

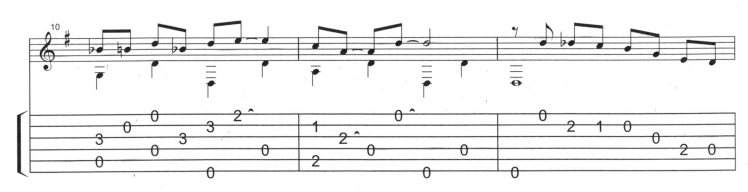

Used by Permission

Jerry Silverman

The many facets of Jerry Silverman's musical background and experience have combined to make him one of this country's most prolific authors of music books. It was his research for his master's thesis in musicology (on blues guitar technique) at New York University that launched him on his musical literary career. Since the publication of his first book, Folk Blues, in 1958, he has authored well over 100 titles, including method books on all levels for guitar, banjo, fiddle, and recorder, as well as American and international songbooks with piano and guitar accompaniment. In addition, Mr. Silverman maintains an active teaching and performing schedule.

Memphis Blues

In 1909, W. C. Handy's band was hired to boost the campaign of Edward H. Crump, who was running for mayor of Memphis. Handy dusted off an anti-Crump song, which soon became the hit tune of the election. Crump was elected and eventually got a boulevard leading to the Mississippi River named after him.

Yellow Dog Blues

*"We dusted off the old number that I had written under the title of **Yellow Dog Rag** and republished it as **Yellow Dog Blues**...A few weeks later a Texan wrote that he had sold more **Yellow Dog Blues** records than anything in the history of his business which he had conducted from the beginning of the phonograph industry." (W.C. Handy)*

The "Yellow Dog" is the Yazoo Delta Railroad.

Been in the Pen So Long

Guitar Solo

Memphis Blues

Guitar Solo

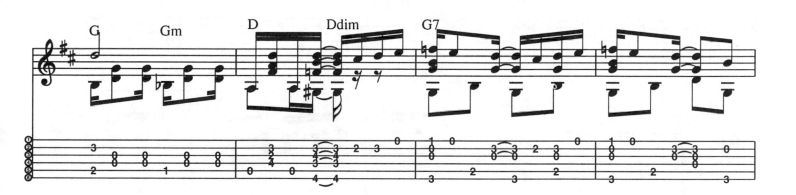

179

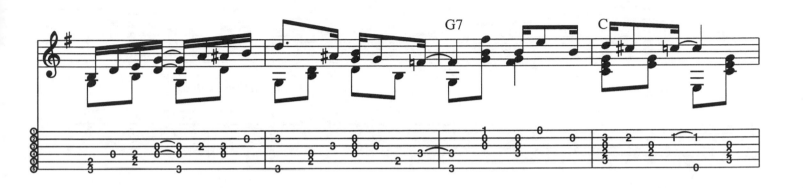

Yellow Dog Blues

Guitar Solo

182

Martin Simpson

English acoustic guitar virtuoso Martin Simpson has come a long way from his roots in Lincolnshire, Northern England. He played his first paid gig at fourteen, became professional at seventeen, and shortly after found himself in the vanguard on British folk-rock movement. He has performed with such musical luminaries as Richard Thompson, Steeleye Span and Fairport Convention, as well as working in the Albion Band and for ten years as collaborator and accompanist with June Tabor. More recently he has shared stages with Steve Miller and David Lindley, as well as recording with Ronnie Earl, Bob Brozman, Ed Gerhard and the Chinese pipe player Wu-Man. He continues to record and tour both solo and with his wife Jessica Ruby Simpson.

Martin's dynamic solo guitar performances are legendary, showcasing his mastery of the acoustic guitar as well as his far-ranging repertoire. He possesses a seemingly effortless command of multiple complex styles, including powerful percussive techniques, unique frailing and fingerstyles, and a ground breaking use of open tunings.

New Kitchen Blues

Tuning: DADGBE

M. Simpson

VERSE A

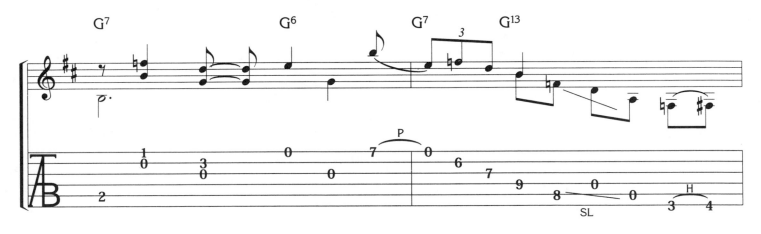

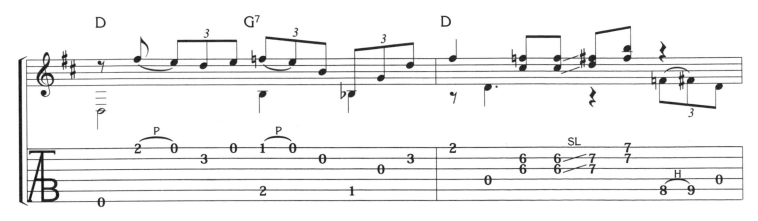

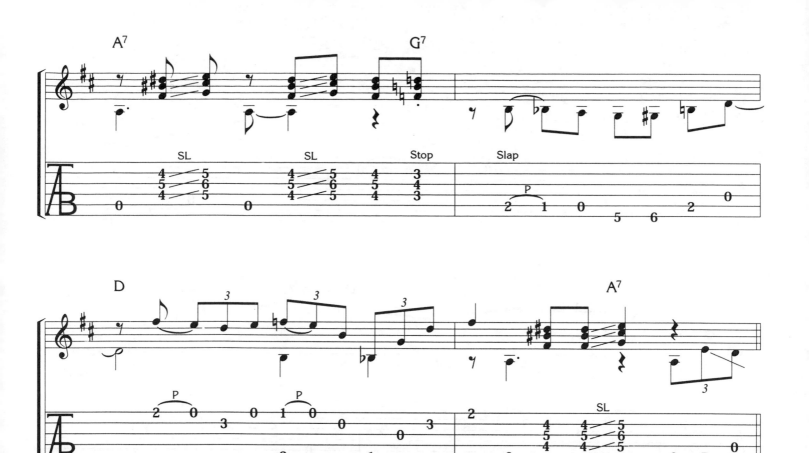

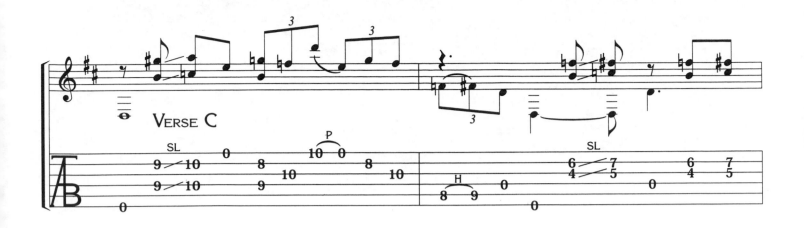

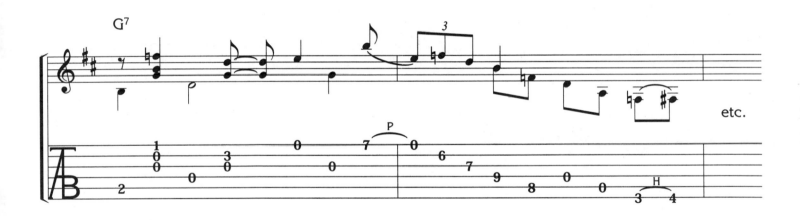

Fred Sokolow

Fred Sokolow is a versatile "musician's musician." A veteran jazz guitarist and singer, he is also an accomplished performer on the 5-string banjo, resonator guitar, and mandolin. Apart from his solo career, Fred has fronted his own jazz, bluegrass, and rock bands, and he has toured with notable performers such as Bobbie Gentry, Jim Stafford, and the Limeliters. In the recording studio, Sokolow has two recordings that showcase his talents. He has written more than 50 instructional guitar and banjo books, tapes and videos for seven major publishers. His books on jazz, rock, country and blues guitar styles are sold on six continents. Other guitar books and videos by Fred Sokolow include: *Beginner's Blues Guitar*-video (MB95208VX), *Best of Blues Guitar* (MB94138BCD), *Learn to Play Bottleneck Guitar* (MB94571BCD), and *Rockabilly Guitar* - video (MB95213VX).

Furry's Train

Furry's Train is reminiscent of the playing of Furry Lewis, who grew up in Memphis, recorded during the '20s, and made a comeback in the '60s. He appeared in a Burt Reynolds movie and was the subject of a '70s Joni Mitchell song.

Like many of Lewis' tunes, this piece is played in open D tuning: D A D F♯ A D (starting with the 6th string). The 12-string guitar used on this recording is tuned a half-step low (12-string guitars are often tuned a fret or two lower than 6-strings), so the tune is really in D♭. The rapid fingerpicking style here is one used by many country/blues artists: the thumb picks bass notes rhythmically, on the main beats (downbeats) while the index and middle fingers play melody on the treble strings, both on- and off-beats. This creates a rolling, syncopated effect. The opening bars of the second theme are typical samples of this style.

A bottleneck is used, sparingly, on the 1st string only (sliding up to the 4th and 12th frets). To play the tune, wear the bottleneck on your little finger (pinky) because you'll need the other fingers of your left hand to fret these chords:

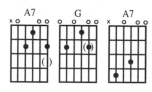

You can sometimes omit the dots in parentheses to get interesting variations of the G and A7 chords. (The second A7 is used momentarily as part of a sliding lick in the first theme.)

You get a D chord in this tuning by strumming open strings.

Mississippi Jump Time

Mississippi Fred McDowell was a very strong bottleneck blues stylist in the Mississippi Delta tradition that produced so many blues giants: Son House, Bukka White, Charlie Patton, Robert Johnson, Muddy Waters...the list goes on. This tune is in that tradition and has some Fred McDowell sounds and licks.

McDowell was "discovered" by Alan Lomax in 1959, and spent his latter years recording and performing to enthusiastic audiences. The Rolling Stones virtually duplicated his version of "You Got To Move" in their '70s recording of the tune.

He used a piece of pipe for a bottleneck, which he wore on his middle finger, and he used his ring and little fingers for fretting. Except for the C7 chord in Jump Time, notice that there is very little fretting except with the bottleneck. The C and D chords are straight bars, which can be done with the bottleneck. The fingerpicking style is standard: fingers pick melody on treble strings while the thumb sometimes beats away at the low G/5th string on downbeats (low D/6th string during a D chord) or alternates on the 5th and 4th strings. Here are the chords:

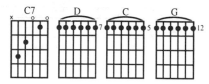

The piece is in open G tuning, often used by McDowell: D G D G B D.

191

Furry's Train

Fast, rolling

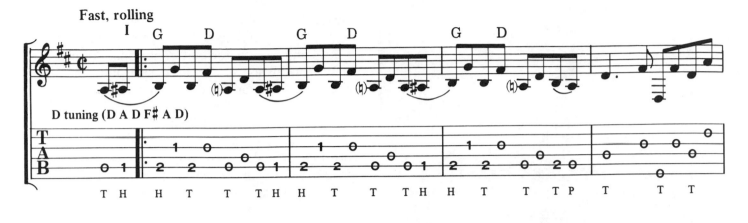

D tuning (D A D F♯ A D)

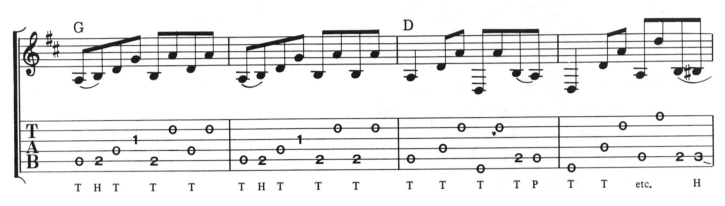

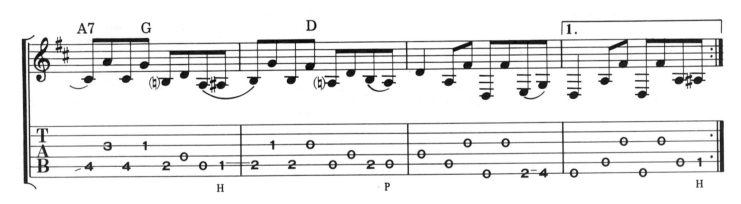

Variation of I (1st 4 bars)

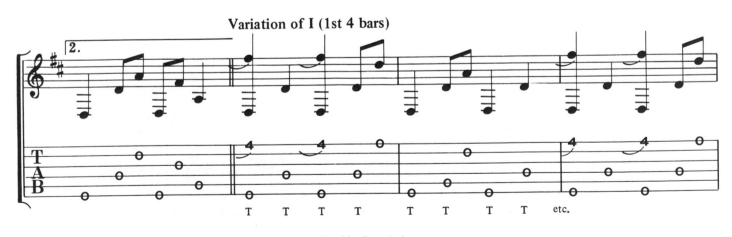

Used by Permission

192

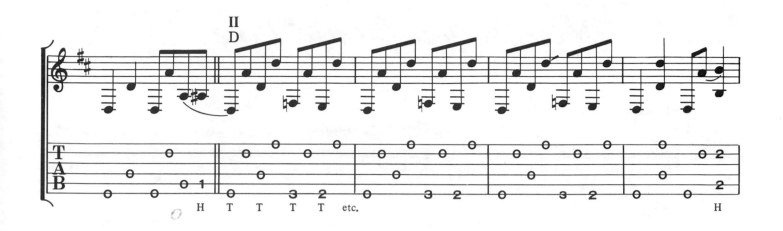

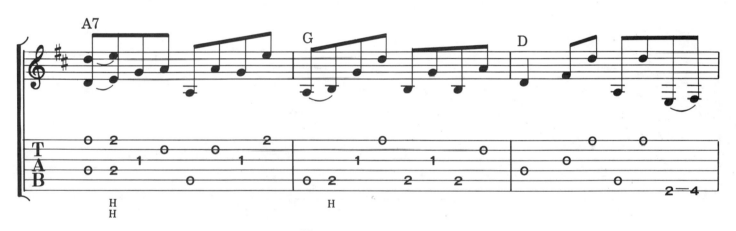

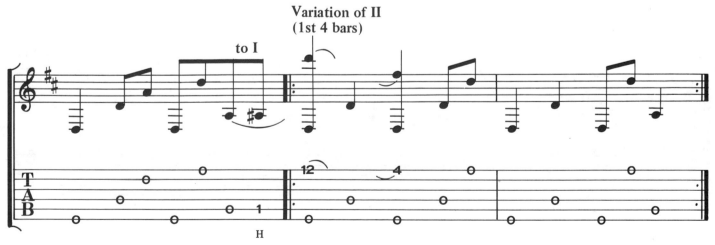

193

Mississippi Jump Time

Fast, bouncy

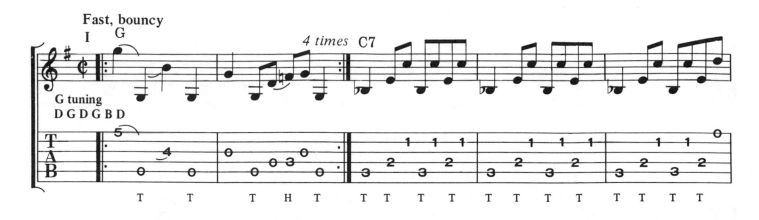

Used by Permission

194

Variation #1
Opening phrase (I)

4 times

Ending:

195

Stanley Solow

Stanley Solow, instructor of guitar at Hofstra University, Hempstead, New York 1966-1986 and Nassau Community College, Garden City, New York 1970 to the present.

A resident of New York City, where he attended Public School 44 (Bronx); Dewitt Clinton High School, and Columbia University. Served in U.S. Army 1942-45 with 445 AAA Bn., 8th Inf. Div.

Married to Rescue Lady Freda; two loving children, Paula Nan (Mrs. Bruce) Watkins, and French hornist Harold Tobias, and their families.

What a Friend We Have In Jesus

Jazz Ballad
Standard Tuning

Charles C. Converse
Arr. John Standefer

Chorus 1   rubato

Used by Permission

Jay Umble

Jay has devoted his life to the study and performance of the guitar. He has studied extensively with world-renowned guitarist, Pat Martino and has released two recordings which incorporate straight-ahead and modern jazz styles. He serves on the faculty of Bucknell University and Susquehanna University as a guitar instructor. Jay writes a monthly jazz guitar column for the Central Pennsylvania "Friends of Jazz" newsletter and performs regularly in Central Pennsylvania with his jazz trio and quartet.

Blue Line

Notes:

1. *Blue Line has a jazz swing feel*
2. *8th notes are generally played as jazz 8ths as opposed to straight 8ths.*
3. *It would be highly technical to list all of the chords used throughout Blue Line. Therefore, the essential chords have been listed to help the learning process.*
4. *Blue Line is easily adapted to larger ensembles—duo, trio, quartet.*

Blue Line

**SOLO GUITAR
(MEDIUM)**

Jay Umble

Used by Permission

215

216

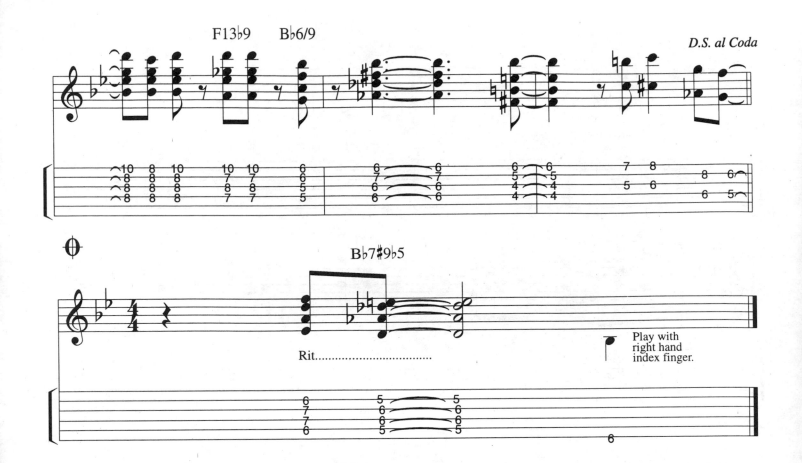

Rit....................................

Play with
right hand
index finger.

218

Phil Upchurch

Born July 19, 1941, in Chicago, Phil Upchurch has been playing professionally since the age of 16 and began his recording career in 1958 at the age of 17 with people like Curtis Mayfield, Otis Rush, and Jimmy Reed.

Phil has gone on to play on thousands of commercials and albums for products and artists of every genre. He has recorded 16 albums of his own as a solo artist. He spent six years (1975-1981) touring and recording with George Benson.

George has recorded three of Phil's compositions. *6 to 4* was recorded on the multi platinum-selling album *Breezin'* and is to this day the largest-selling jazz album in history.

In 1985 Phil taught himself to read music through the study of Segovia's guitar transcriptions and has added MIDI guitar and computer technology to his wide repetoire of instruments. He is also a much-recorded bassist and has been sought out to play bass as well as guitar on the same sessions by many producers.

B's Shuffle

Phil Upchurch

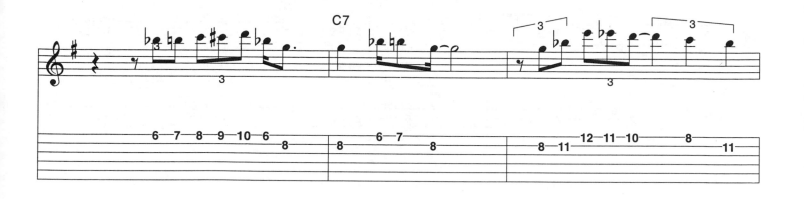

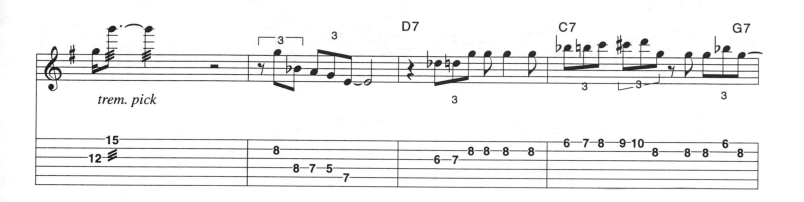

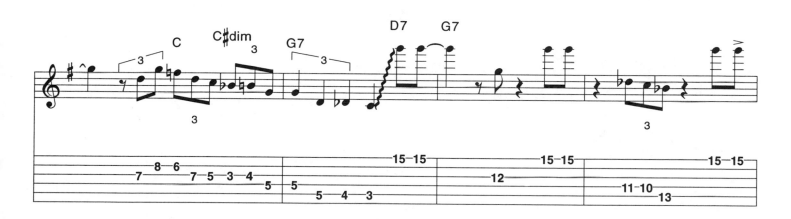

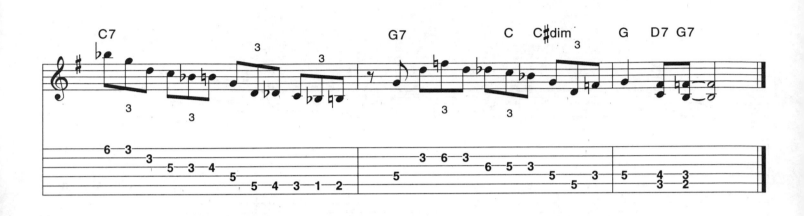

222

Paul Yandell

Photo by Douglas G. Cochran

Yandell is semi-retired, but still finds time to work on projects such as the Branding video, *Paul Yandell, Fingerstyle Legacy,* and work with Chet Atkins. At one time, he was active as a session player, performing and recording with Hank Thompson, Kitty Wells, Perry Como, Roger Whittaker, Dolly Parton, and on movie soundtracks including *Tender Mercies* and *Every Which Way But Loose.* But Yandell tired of the work when the business began to change. Says Yandell, "In country music, they won't play anything recorded before '86–before Randy Travis. It's like nobody ever lived before then. The program directors don't worry about what the public wants. They're like the government–they know what's best for you. Besides, everybody wants to play like Albert Lee nowadays. I can't play like Albert Lee. As far as the record business is concerned, thumbstyle guitar playing is about as popular as '61 Chevys. You see one now and then, but most of them are rusty."

As for his days on the road, Yandell comments, "People think it's exciting, but everybody just thinks about getting back home. The best time you have is that hour and a half that you spend on stage. That's where all the fun is. It's not the going and a-coming–that's what wears your butt out. It's better, though, than hauling gravel or working in a tobacco patch!"

Yandell's successes can be attributed to the practice of old fashioned adages. "Listen to everybody else does and try to be different," he says. "If you ever hear any good advice, take it. All I ever want to do when I was a kid was to come to Nashville and play at the Grand Ole' Opry. That was my dream night and day. And the dream eventually came true. Over the years, I've had the opportunities to record with Chet, Les Paul, Jerry Reed. I've played with Merle, Lenny Beau–all my heroes. What more could a guy want? I've really been lucky just to be friends with people like that. And if I can make it, just about anybody can, because I'm just an average talent–not bad, not great, just somewhere in between. Just believe in yourself and try hard enough. Who knows? You might be able to get a job with somebody like Chet."

Clear Spring Blues

The road that runs past my mother's house where I was born and raised is called Clear Springs Road. What could be a better title?

Clear Spring Blues

Transcribed by
Craig Dobbins

Paul Yandell

224

* tremelo strum with
pad of finger

John Zaradin

Photo by Laurence Burns

John Zaradin is Europe's foremost player of classical Brazilian guitar music. His early training at the Royal College of Music and the Paris Conservatoire has combined with his deep involvement and love of the music and people of South America, to result in the unique sound he makes today.

John Zaradin holds a Gold Disc for his recording of the Rodrigo Concerto de Aranjuez on EMI's Classics For Pleasure, having sold over a quarter million copies. His other recordings of classical guitar music have included works by Vivaldi, Buxtehude, Cimarosa, Bach and Scarlatti.

After his formal training in London and Paris as a pupil of Alexander Lagoya, John Zaradin began composing and performing his own guitar music on both classical and Brazilian styles. His numerous works are currently published by Belwin-Mills and Hampton Guitar Music including the recent index of rhythm patterns - *A Unique Approach To The Study Of Rhythm*. John Zaradin has given live television and radio performances in the major musical centers of all five continents.

Over the years, John Zaradin has fused European formality with the spontaneity of Latin America, especially Brazil. His music has been played in concerts with John Dankworth, Paco Pena and other musicians. Brazilian music is now regarded as a valuable source of inspiration to contemporary composers in the same way that European folk music was to such composers as Bartok, Dvorak, and Brahms.

Dubuque Blues

This piece, as a 12 bar blues, features a "walking bass line" idea. Improvising and maintaining a bass line is a great feature for the fingerstyle guitar but requires practice until the player knows the chord changes and bass line by instinct.

In practicing the style, start by working out some variations on the patterns of the chord shapes that the left handing is holding. With patience and practice you can build up your own repertoire of arpeggios and scale lines that can be introduced at will. Eventually you will find yourself creating spontaneously over the changes.

Dubuque Blues

John Zaradin

Used by Permission